# Gardening the Earth
## gateways to a sustainable future

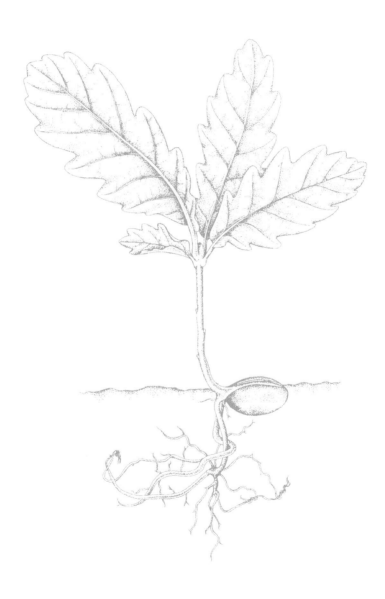

## Stephen Blackmore
Regius Keeper, Royal Botanic Garden Edinburgh

Royal
Botanic Garden
Edinburgh

To my family

First published 2009 by the Royal Botanic Garden
Edinburgh, Inverleith Row, Edinburgh, EH3 5LR

978-1-906129-19-4    Paperback edition
978-1-906129-20-0    Hardback edition

Printed by: Scotprint, Scotland

The Guiana Highlands of Venezuela, a biodiversity hotspot where
precipitous 'tepuis' or table mountains rise from the tropical forest.
Image: Stephen Blackmore.

# Gardening the Earth
## gateways to a sustainable future

Royal
Botanic Garden
Edinburgh

# CONTENTS

A classic Chinese garden landscape frames distant views of nature: Yulong Xue Shan, or Jade Dragon Snow Mountain, towers above Heilong Tan, the Black Dragon Pool, built during the Qing Dynasty in 1737. At 3,200m on the flank of the mountain is the Jade Dragon Field Station. Image: Stephen Blackmore.

CLARENCE HOUSE

Gardens offer a vision of an ideal world where people work the soil to the rhythm of the seasons, in harmonious balance with Nature. However, it is now clearly apparent that the natural world, on which all human existence depends, is threatened as never before. The threats include climate change and the over-exploitation or degradation of many critical eco-systems, on land and at sea. These eco-systems, and the immense biodiversity they support, provide services essential to our continued existence on this planet, although most of the time we are unaware of them and take them for granted. So it really is imperative that we find a way of revitalising the ancient and timeless view that Mankind has a duty of stewardship over natural resources, before it is too late. And I fear the clock is ticking ever faster…

Climate change is without doubt the biggest threat we face. It will cause dramatic changes to all our lives, far beyond the consequences – which are already becoming apparent – for those of us who cherish our gardens in this still green and pleasant land. Yet understanding the scale of the challenges we will face in our own gardens may perhaps help us to comprehend the wider, and potentially appalling, implications of climate change for all of humanity. This, in turn, might encourage us to take responsible action to limit the damage, while there is still just time to do so. As I write this, and according to the available science, we have only 98 months left as a window in which we can take the necessary action to avert catastrophic climate change and 98 months pass by very quickly, I can assure you.

I am delighted that Professor Blackmore has somehow found time to write this book. It presents an important vision of how we might rediscover our rightful place in the natural order and I hope it will bring every reader down to earth, seized with the need to face the future with practical action. There are many things we can do, starting with joining the campaign to halt tropical deforestation before we lose what is in effect the world's "air-conditioning system", providing us, apart from anything else, with the vital rainfall we all need for growing crops and for our very survival.

As Patron of the Royal Botanic Garden Edinburgh and Botanic Gardens Conservation International (BGCI), I am immensely proud of the part botanic gardens play in helping to conserve the diversity of plants that support all life on Earth and which are currently being made extinct at an unprecedented rate. This book offers a timely reminder that effective collective action depends on a myriad of individual choices. As gardeners, we are closer to the natural order of things than most of our fellow citizens. Each one of us can and must take responsibility for the future of the living world. If we don't, future generations will surely demand to know why not.

**Above:** Kingcups, *Caltha palustris*. Image: Stephen Blackmore.

# INTRODUCTION

The Chiquibul Forest Reserve extends over half a million hectares and, as the largest protected area in Belize, is home to jaguars, scarlet macaws and a huge diversity of plants despite extensive settlement by the ancient Maya and logging for mahogany in the 20th century. The clearing in the forest is the Las Cuevas Research Station. Image: Stephen Blackmore

Running pell-mell. Hurtling headlong downhill towards a patch of shining gold by the brook with its sticklebacks, caddis flies and bully heads. Golden sun shines from petals, reflecting in a field of green. Kingcups! Fit for a king, they outshine mere buttercups. Buttercups are for milkmaids and for seeing who likes butter. Kingcups are for kings. Brightest in the wide world, they catch my attention, shining by the brook.

"Come on!" It's time to run again. Across the brook on a bridge of railway sleepers. No time to look for eggs in the blackbird's nest hiding in the dog rose.

Everything in the world has its name and its place. Everything has its way of growing and living. Some people know the names and way of things but most don't. Strange - they remember the colours of every football team but can't tell kingcups from buttercups. Yet, if you don't know the names of things you can find them in an Observer's Book.

I got the Observer's Book of Pond Life for my birthday and now I know that the strange inky-blue shells I found are freshwater pearl mussels (Margaritifera margaritifera) and I know they are not common. The people who wrote the Observer's Books have seen everything in the big wide world. One day I want to be one of them. I want to be a naturalist and write books about the names and places of things. But not yet, not now while there's kingcups, newts, ragged robin, caddis fly larvae, freshwater pearl mussels and bully heads...

...Today, all the species of my childhood haunts are still there, somewhere, although some are much scarcer now. The bullhead fish (*Cottus gobio)*, or bully head as we called them, is now a threatened species, listed in Annex II of the European Commission Habitats Directive. The freshwater pearl mussel is in decline in the UK and now has a Species Action Plan intended to support its recovery. Luckily for me, it turned out that it was possible to become a botanist and my horizons soon expanded from the fields and moors of Staffordshire. My library had begun with birthday and Christmas presents from my parents: the *Observer's Book of Wild Animals* and *Birds* when I was seven; *Butterflies* at nine; *Pond Life* and *The Sea and Seashore* when I was 11. For the names of plants I used my mother's copy of *Wayside and Woodland Plants.* I still treasure them all. Soon, tropical field guides joined them on the shelves as I ventured further and further from the back brook. In those days I kept to myself my ambition of becoming a naturalist and writing books for fear of scorn; even at school it was clear that nature was just for children. What strikes me today is that my childhood was surrounded by a dazzling diversity of living things. Are children growing up today so fortunate? Perhaps they are not at liberty to roam as far and wide as I did in those more innocent times. But if they had such freedom, would they find the wonders I did? Sadly nature has been on the retreat for the last half-century and now seems the right time to write a book I never dreamed necessary as a boy.

What is there to say about the world of nature that has not been said already? I want to celebrate the beautiful planet we are fortunate to live upon but also to explore the enormous challenges of environmental change. Ours is a planet brimming with life. It has evolved an extraordinary abundance and variety of living things, including vast numbers of species that have yet to be recognised and documented. Until we have explored it more completely, the living planet that we are part of remains more complex than we can possibly imagine. It is this very complexity that is slipping through our fingers in ways that would be difficult enough to tackle even if nothing else was changing. But on a greenhouse planet, humankind's

steady erosion of living diversity is greatly compounded by climate change.

I do not have all the answers and do not suggest that there are any quick or easy solutions. The complexity of both the challenges themselves and the myriad interconnections in the web of life rule out any simplistic solutions. It is apparent how little more there is to say when one considers the prescience of past pioneers such as John Muir, Patrick Geddes and Aldo Leopold along with more recent works

**Above**: The budding botanist in the 1950s: "I ran wild in the fields behind our back garden, returning with flowers to press or trophies to display in the 'museum' shed." Image: Edwin Arthur Blackmore.

**Right**: Plants for our planet. Image: RBGE/Debbie White.

**Below**: Old habits die hard: the adult botanist at work on Aldabra Atoll in 2003 with plant press and giant tortoise. Image: Stephen Blackmore.

by Jared Diamond, James Lovelock, Edward O. Wilson and a host of others. However, since childhood I have soaked up ideas about nature like a sponge. I hope at least to bring some freshness to the topic by presenting it as a personal perspective.

Having travelled widely, and having the privilege of being Regius Keeper at the Royal Botanic Garden Edinburgh, over the years I have formulated ideas about possible solutions to the challenges we face. In particular, I have a strong belief in the remarkable contribution botanic gardens can make both through

direct action to protect plants as the basis of life and in their catalytic role of engaging and motivating people. I also want to share my sense of optimism that our intelligent and imaginative species, once alert to the challenges ahead, can do what needs to be done to secure the best future.

What we must do, above all else, is keep our rich biological inheritance. We need to inhabit a green, living world in which the global ecosystem maintains its capacity to meet our needs and those of other living things. Doing this means finding a more sustainable relationship with the natural world and, I suggest, the speediest route to that destination is to think in the way that gardeners do. Gardeners are well suited to being the stewards of the planet. As Patrick Geddes said, "A garden is the very best of Savings Banks for, in return for deposits of time and strength, otherwise largely wasted, the worker reaps health for himself and his children in air, vegetables and in fruit." Gardening the Earth might turn out to be the best way of safeguarding our future.

**Below**: The majestic Redwood Avenue at Benmore Botanic Garden, a fine example of long-term thinking. Image: RBGE/ Lynsey Wilson.

## The mindset of the gardener

Gardening provides an appropriate philosophy for tackling the environmental challenges facing the Earth. If we managed our planet as we do our gardens, we might have reason to be more confident about the future. The mindset of the gardener has six great strengths:

1. **Long-term thinking.** The gardener works to shape a small part of the world according to a long-term design they might not live to see. This is especially true when it comes to planting trees – in itself a commitment to the future.
2. **Vision.** There is a vision of the future garden in mind, whether it is a place of inspiration and reflection, a collection of medicinal plants, a favourite group of plants, or even a re-creation of the world in miniature. To achieve their vision the gardener does not stand back and let things happen, they intervene in nature, to favour one species over another.
3. **Connection.** Gardening involves a deep sense of connection with place; an intense, purposeful engagement quite different from the way we often take the world as a whole for granted.
4. **Recycling.** Gardeners are the ultimate recyclers, distributing spare plants to friends and neighbours and turning surplus ones and waste into compost to improve the soil.
5. **Determination.** Gardeners are not put off easily. If they do not succeed at first, they are inclined to try again. Weeds may be persistent but gardeners are determined, sometimes to the point of stubbornness.
6. **Responsibility.** The gardener accepts responsibility for their patch; they don't expect someone else to do all the hard work for them. We need to accept similar responsibility for the entire planet.

A garden is not nature but it can be a reflection of nature and in our increasingly urbanised world it is often the best substitute for nature. A garden is a small ecosystem; managed carefully it can be home to many species of animals as well as plants. It can represent a microcosm of the world and also provide a metaphor for the way we should care for the planet.

Image: Stephen Blackmore.

*Trees cling to rocky bluffs and steep-sided burns inaccessible to deer on the slopes of Beinn Sgritheall overlooking Arnisdale and Loch Hourn. Beyond lies Knoydart, now in the care of the John Muir Trust. Forest was once much more extensive in the Highlands but thanks to ambitious projects like the Millennium Forest for Scotland, isolated groups of trees can once again re-seed the landscape.*

# PART 1:

Fire can be a destructive force but in the tropical palm savannas of
Belize it is a natural and frequent event to which the native plants are

CHAPTER 1

## ALL THE WORLD'S A GARDEN

*"All the world's a stage,*
*And all the men and women merely players;*
*They have their exits and entrances;*
*And one man in his time plays many parts…"*

William Shakespeare's lines from *As You Like It* have been
understood in many ways and adopted for a wide variety of
purposes. Usually they are considered to reflect the much
earlier concept of the 'Theatrum Mundi' in which human life
is simply an amusement for the gods. Accordingly, life follows
a predetermined course and must progress through the seven
ages from infancy to "second childishness and mere oblivion".

I have appropriated Shakespeare's words and turned them to
a different purpose. All the world's a garden because nowhere
on Earth is now truly a wilderness, beyond the reach of
human influence. Throughout history we have relied upon
nature, first as hunter gatherers, then as farmers and now as
city dwellers. Now nature must rely on us. If we choose to
act as gardeners of the Earth we may yet deliver the world
from the mere oblivion that now threatens to be its fate.

# WHAT ON EARTH HAVE WE DONE?

We know, because almost every day newspapers and the broadcast media tell us, that the world faces an environmental crisis. But what exactly is the problem? In a nutshell, the planet is now so completely dominated by us and so wounded by our demands upon it that it no longer works as it once did.

To understand how this came about we need to stand back and try to see the world as a whole, perhaps taking the perspective of the Apollo astronauts, the only people to have visited another world. If we were sitting in a deckchair on the moon, looking dispassionately at the Earth from afar, we might note with

**Facing page**: The title page from John Gerard's *The Herball, or Generall Historie of Plantes*, (first published in 1597), 1633 edition, showing John Gerard, English herbalist. Image: RBGE/Lynsey Wilson.

**Left**: Earth from the moon, as seen by the Apollo 11 astronauts in 1969. Our living planet seems surprisingly small and so different from anything else in the solar system. Image courtesy of NASA/JSC scan.

**Below**: Growing concern: newspaper headlines testify to the environmental crisis.

**Above**: A reconstruction of a creature resembling a giant wombat *(Diprotodon optatum)*, which existed in Australia 50,000 years ago. The two metre tall marsupial would have been hunted extensively for its meat, though Australian scientists also cite climate change as one of the reasons for its demise. Image: © Anne Musser.

surprise how small the planet is and how unlike anything else we can see. The main signal our instrument array would detect is a recent warming of the planet, associated with changes in the composition of its atmosphere.

Climate change is the most obvious symptom of a fevered Earth. In the century between 1905 and 2005 global temperatures rose by an average of 0.6°C. During the same period the average amount of carbon dioxide in the atmosphere increased by about a third and is rising rapidly. Through the 21st century, if greenhouse gases continue to increase as predicted, we could see a further 2°C rise in temperatures. We will return to the real-life significance of these changes later in the book. But climate change has the added effect of magnifying and multiplying the planet's other man-made woes. We will see how, as its numbers multiplied, one dominant species reshaped the natural ecosystems of the planet to meet its needs, straining resources of land and water, displacing other species and precipitating a mass extinction. In short, humans have taken two crucial actions leading to a rapid increase in atmospheric carbon dioxide: deforesting large tracts of land and exploiting vast deposits of fossil fuels.

*A ravenous species reshaped the landscape*

The root cause is to be found a long time ago. *Homo sapiens* emerged in Africa, some 200,000 years ago on a continent rich in natural resources. Around 100,000 years ago our ancestors began to migrate out of Africa seeking their fortunes in the wider world. They found a bountiful earth, even at high latitudes and high elevations. Although their numbers were low, their impact was significant, especially on the largest animals of each new land and continent they entered. Around the world large herbivores such as mammoths, the woolly rhinoceros and the giant sloth became extinct and with them went predators like the sabre-toothed tiger that were unaccustomed to having to share their prey. It was no accident that early humans hunted large herbivores, depriving their predators of food. Why not seek out the most plentiful places to take the largest and easiest prey? And why not hunt until none remained? It was no more likely that our earliest ancestors would have established national parks to conserve the mammoths than that sheep would agree to set aside the grazing on one side of their field. Only one continent on Earth retained a full diversity of large herbivores and their predators: Africa. In the cradle of human life the story of our early ancestors ran alongside that of the other animals and a balance was struck that endured, just about, until fairly recently.

Forty thousand years ago humans had dispersed into the Middle East, Europe, the Arctic and had even reached New Guinea and Australia. In North America, humans arrived across the Bering Strait from Asia about 13,500 years ago and found a huge diversity of large mammals, a ready resource for hunting. As recently as 350 BC, the first human colonists reached Madagascar and dined on giant birds and giant reptiles: the elephant bird and the giant tortoise. When the Maoris reached New Zealand, perhaps only as recently as 1280 AD, they found not large mammals but the flightless moa birds. Mammals, birds and reptiles fuelled the march of humans across the Earth. Each animal was itself sustained by photosynthetic plants, harnessing the energy of the sun. But plants did not escape the attention of early humans either. Trees were felled for fire and shelters. When people moved into a neighbourhood it changed, and it changed forever.

Once our ancestors had used up the immediate resources of large animals, they generally settled into a longer-term relationship with their new lands, shaping them according to their needs. It is difficult to argue that they improved upon what they had found. In each continent a parallel progression from hunter-gatherer to cultivator took place. Peoples around the world worked out ways of life that were largely in harmony with nature, allowing the long-term survival of the animals and plants they domesticated and depended upon. Such a balance was achieved quite easily when the human population was small and widely dispersed, which it was for most of human history.

Our domination of nature began in earnest some 15,000 years ago when our ancestors began to domesticate animals and plants. We developed different forms of agriculture on the different continents, we began to establish

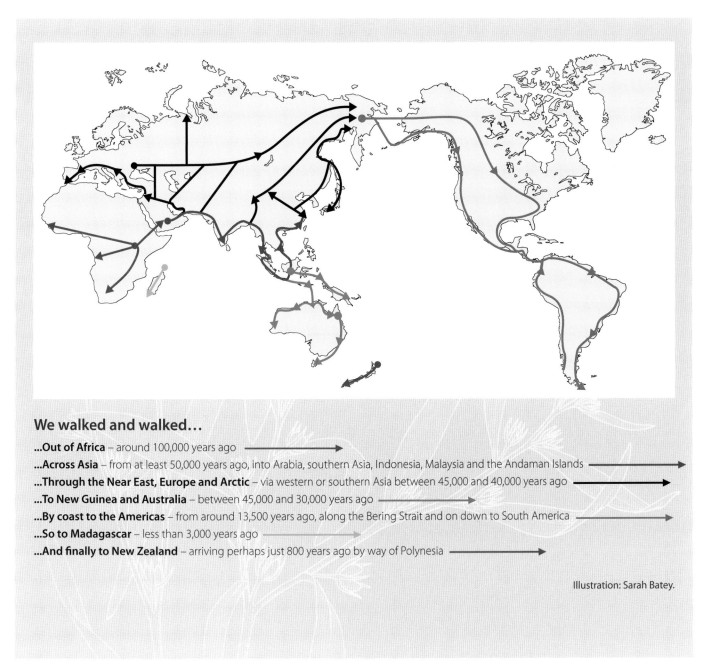

## We walked and walked...

**...Out of Africa** – around 100,000 years ago

**...Across Asia** – from at least 50,000 years ago, into Arabia, southern Asia, Indonesia, Malaysia and the Andaman Islands

**...Through the Near East, Europe and Arctic** – via western or southern Asia between 45,000 and 40,000 years ago

**...To New Guinea and Australia** – between 45,000 and 30,000 years ago

**...By coast to the Americas** – from around 13,500 years ago, along the Bering Strait and on down to South America

**...So to Madagascar** – less than 3,000 years ago

**...And finally to New Zealand** – arriving perhaps just 800 years ago by way of Polynesia

Illustration: Sarah Batey.

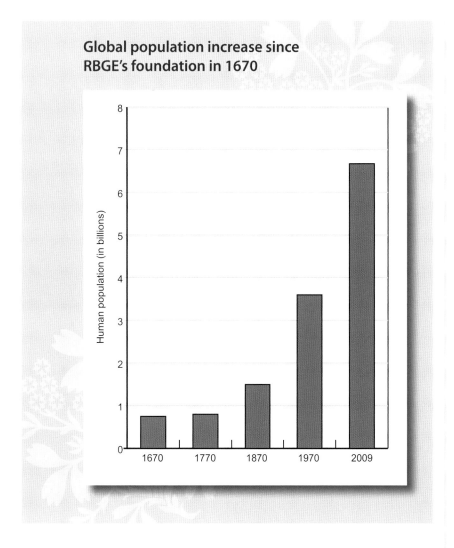

**Global population increase since RBGE's foundation in 1670**

*Human population (in billions)*

(Bar chart showing population values for years 1670, 1770, 1870, 1970, 2009)

**Above**: For thousands of years before the origin of the Royal Botanic Garden Edinburgh in 1670, the human population remained below one billion. In the last century it doubled twice and now stands at 6.6 billion. Recently, the United Nations predicted that the world population will reach 7 billion in early 2012 and 9 billion by 2050. Illustration: Sarah Batey.

complex societies that could live in cities, and human numbers started to climb inexorably. Thus, the emergence of recognisable civilisations around the world marked the beginning of the brief but eventful chapter in the Earth's history during which we drastically reduced the primeval forests, greatly impairing the planet's natural capacity for air conditioning. Forests do not just stand. They mediate not only the balance of atmospheric gases but also other fundamental processes including soil formation and the water cycle. The retreat of the forests has altered the balance of the planet. If forests are, as some say, the lungs of the Earth, then we humans had already removed one lung before we even began our great modern expansion.

## Surviving on one lung

When in the late 1700s the sound of the steam engine began to be heard more frequently, many of the world's forests had long since been consumed, its wetlands had been drained and growing numbers of people flourished. Slowly and steadily new, distinctive and relatively stable landscapes emerged – agricultural landscapes shaped by human activities. Even today we think of them as the countryside but these familiar landscapes contain only a selected subset of the species that might once have lived there.

It was not until the middle of the 1800s that the global population passed the one billion mark. The chances are that your great-great-grandparents knew this world. Supporting so many people placed a considerable burden on the planet, with human activities accounting for an increasing proportion of all the energy that photosynthesising plants could capture from the sun. In all the cradles of human civilisation – in the Middle East, in parts of Asia and in Europe – forests had long since given way to agricultural fields and pastures. Humans began to use the products of ancient as well as present photosynthesis, exploiting fossil fuels, especially coal, in addition to timber.

By the time the Industrial Revolution began in Europe, up to half of the world's original forests, those that were present when our species emerged and into which we dispersed, had already vanished. It is difficult to conceive how much impact this had on the planet and on its capacity to maintain the natural cycles of atmospheric gases and water or the development of soils. We evolved as forest dwellers but began to love the wide open spaces and to fear the dark interior of the forest.

In some parts of the world, marked changes in climate were already apparent before the Industrial Revolution. The Middle East, the birthplace of European civilisations, was much drier; the lush, evergreen forests that had surrounded the Mediterranean shrank to isolated patches on Atlantic islands. On the other side of the world, the centre of Australia dried out. Meanwhile a lush monsoonal savanna of 10,000 years ago that is now the Sahara desert began to dry, forcing humans to abandon the region

## Origins of agriculture

More than 13,000 years ago humans on several continents began to switch from gathering food from the wild to settling and growing crops. Our picture of this process, painstakingly established by archaeologists, is patchy and incomplete. It must have been a gradual progression but is widely seen as the turning point that allowed complex civilisations to emerge.

In Asia, cultivation of rice began some 13,000 years ago at about the same time as cultivation of rye in the Middle East. Wheat and barley can be traced back 10,000 years to northwest India and the Middle East and around this time maize began to be cultivated in Mexico. Other familiar crops including cotton, cassava, beans, figs, peanuts and squashes have at least 10,000 years history of cultivation. Today three cereals – wheat, rice and maize – remain the most important staple foods followed by potato, cassava, soybean, barley and sweet potato. Around the world more than 7,000 species of plants from a wide variety of families form part of the human diet.

**Above:** Yi minority farmers ploughing in Yunnan, China.

Image: Stephen Blackmore.

8,000 years ago. People returned briefly some 4,500 years ago but were forced to leave when the climate became even drier. Did changes in climate cause the forests to retreat or did human activities including forest clearance cause the rains to fail? Although each explanation has its advocates, I do not think it is meaningful to try to separate cause and effect in this case. It is just an early example of how our fate has always been intertwined with that of Earth's climate and its forests.

## Ultimate invaders, ultimate survivors

Since our species evolved and spread across the world it has had to contend with many calamities, including the last Ice Age which ended just 10,000 years ago. We coped. But back then we lived in small, self-sufficient groups of hunter-gatherers or early farmers. When life became unbearable in one place we moved somewhere better. One way or another we got everywhere. Let us not be bashful: we were clever and creative. We found ways of living almost everywhere, however hot or cold the climate. The Inuit and the Australian Aboriginal show as clearly as any other contemporary society the human ability to find a way of life that works anywhere on planet Earth.

Humanity has faced many challenges along the way, including famine, pestilence and war. Now we face global challenges greater than anything in our history. The depletion of the protective ozone layer in the Earth's atmosphere is just one example of the truly global reach of human activities. As the ultimate survivors, once we recognised the threat of the ozone layer hole we began to deal with it through unprecedented international efforts. Today other threats impinge on our consciousnesses with increasing urgency. The oceans are

## Resilient nature

The Maya Forest straddling three neighbouring countries – Belize, Mexico and Guatemala – bears the influence of two distinct waves of human occupation and shows how nature can restore itself in time, if all the pieces are to hand.

The ancient Mayan civilisation spread widely through the region from around 1800 BC, raising spectacular ceremonial cities like Tikal, Caracol and Chichen Itza before abandoning them suddenly around 900 AD. Tropical forests reclaimed a once heavily occupied landscape. At the height of the Classic Maya civilisation Belize, with a present day population of fewer than 300,000, was home to an estimated two million people.

Through the 19th until the mid 20th century selective logging of mahogany for export was the mainstay of the Belizean economy but even this did not displace the tapir, scarlet macaw, jaguar and four other species of native cat. In the 1990s I was involved with others, including Nicodemus 'Chapal' Bol (pictured here, right) in establishing the Las Cuevas Research Station in the most extensive remaining tract of the Maya Forest: the Chiquibul. Research and conservation averted the risk of development. The Chiquibul became recognised as an important biodiversity hotspot and the stronghold of the jaguar in Central America. International efforts are underway to create a Mesoamerican Biological Corridor so plants and animals can migrate through the fragmented forest.

Even tropical forests can recover in time and there is much we can do to accelerate the process.

Image: Stephen Blackmore.

becoming more acidic and plastic residues are widespread in the natural environment. It is still difficult to predict the full range of likely impacts that will result from these changes. In contrast, we understand quite well the impacts of greenhouse gases on global warming and can model the future with a steadily increasing degree of accuracy. The biology of the planet is also undergoing rapid change with both the reduction in abundance of many species and the dramatic increase, in the wrong places, of other species that become invasive. Everywhere is affected. Are we capable of responding as well as our Ice Age ancestors?

Life is not so simple today. Our creativity has enabled us to construct a very complex way of life in a globalised economy. However good at our own jobs we are, we probably don't know how to do many other jobs – how to prepare vaccines, how to make a microprocessor, how to separate the wheat from the chaff, to know what lies beneath the bonnet of a modern motor car? We have become such specialists that almost no one can make a decent flint axe head. It is easy to imagine that we conquered nature long ago and have reorganised the world to be just as we need it. It is possible to inhabit a dream in today's electronic age with its many distractions from reality. At home and at work, we spend almost as much time looking at liquid crystal display screens as we do at the real world. There is a danger that, faced with unprecedented challenges, we will just plump up the cushions and flick through the channels on television. *Homo sapiens* does have the ability to comprehend the world, to tackle the problems it has created and restore a natural balance based on a more sustainable relationship with nature. But first we must acknowledge that we are part of nature and accept that we have pushed our planet to a point of no return. Every inch of the Earth bears our imprint.

The view from the moon is accurate, ours is a small planet. It is a finite world and nowadays none of it is wilderness devoid of human impact. Aldabra, a dot of land in a swirling ocean, reminds us, as does the view from space, that our planet is mainly blue, with its oceans much greater than its landmasses. Blue or green, neither land nor ocean has been unchanged by our species, the ultimate invaders.

## A shrinking world

Nowhere is now truly remote. The village market now connects with the global market. When legendary plant collectors George Forrest (above, left) and Joseph Rock visited Lijiang in Yunnan Province in the first decades of the 20th century, travel was on foot or horseback and they found a diversity of distinct cultures. Today a modern airport and network of trunk roads bring over four million visitors a year to Lijiang from other parts of China. They come to see nature in the mountains and for a glimpse of life in the past through the architecture and customs of the minority people. Started in 2000, the Jade Dragon Field Station stands in a windy pass at 3,200 metres above sea level on what was once part of the Tea Horse Road, an important trade route to Tibet.

Comparison with George Forrest's photographs shows how little the appearance of the Jade Dragon Snow Mountain has changed since his day. The Naxi and Yi peoples still keep their distinctive costumes. But subtle changes have occurred, large trees suitable for constructing houses are now rare on the lower slopes and medicinal plants, once an abundant resource harvested from the wild, are now rare and threatened. The market for traditional Chinese medicines is now a global one extending to every major city around the world and the race is on to protect and increase the wild populations of these and other increasingly threatened plants.

Life in the mountain villages is becoming easier as roads and electricity extend to villages like Wen Hai, home to staff at the Jade Dragon Field Station. But local people are anxious about climate change: the glaciers that feed the many rivers flowing from the mountain are in retreat. Nature has sustained them for thousands of years but what does the future hold?

Image: RBGE archives.

Inhospitable though it looks, Aldabra is home to
extraordinary endemic plants and animals including
some 100,000 giant tortoises.
Image: Stephen Blackmore.

# Aldabra

The most remote place I know well is Aldabra Atoll, an almost uninhabited island situated in the Indian Ocean some 300 miles off the east coast of Africa. I have been fortunate to return several times since I spent my first year as a professional botanist there in the late 1970s. It is a paradise for wildlife including the Aldabran giant tortoise (Geochelone gigantea). There are fewer than a dozen human beings living on the atoll but a short stroll along the strand line on Aldabra soon reveals evidence of the millions living over the horizon. Huge quantities of plastic bottles, sandals, flip flops and other debris of civilised life wash up on the shore every day.

# CHAPTER 2

**Above:** Autumn leaves at RBGE. Image: RBGE/Lynsey Wilson.

## BY LEAVES WE LIVE

*"How many people think twice about a leaf? Yet the leaf is the chief product and phenomenon of life: this is a green world, with animals comparatively few and small, and all dependent on the leaves. By leaves we live. Some people have strange ideas that they live by money. They think energy is generated by the circulation of coins. Whereas the world is mainly a vast leaf colony, growing on and forming a leafy soil, not a mere mineral mass: and we live not by the jingling of our coins, but by the fullness of our harvests."*

These words, spoken by Patrick Geddes, contain a timeless and universal truth that has even greater resonance in the early 21st century. The extent of the world's leaf colony has been greatly reduced. Yet, by leaves we live, still. Every aspect of our existence depends upon plants. Our species could not have evolved until plants had created the air we breathe. They feed, shelter, fuel and cure us and if we want to secure our future we must tend to the leaves. If we become global gardeners, plants will provide for our future.

# WAKING UP TO REALITY

Why have we started to ask questions about the future of the planet and everything that hurtles through space on it? Al Gore called it an inconvenient truth. Its simple name is reality. Now at last there is a new awareness of human impact on the planet. Our species is waking up. We are beginning to realise that the dream of an endless planet designed for our convenience, with an abundance of everything we could possibly need, is merely fantasy. Quite suddenly, in a few short years, we have started to see what we have done to the Earth. This awakening might just turn out to be the most important thing we humans have ever experienced.

How and why has this happened? Some people consider that the publication in 1962 of Rachel Carson's *Silent Spring* marked the beginning of the age of environmental awareness. Certainly it was a book that issued a warning about the unintended consequences of our modern life, with its intensive agriculture and over-dependence on pesticides. Important though *Silent Spring* was, there is a much longer tradition of writing about the place of man in nature. This genre does not have a single starting point, but few would challenge the suggestion that John Muir was a persuasive pioneer who captured the importance of nature and wilderness. Setting forth from Dunbar at the age of 11 in 1849 for a life in the New World, his reach was international and his legacy extraordinary. Muir wrote of his simple childhood pleasures, finding bird's nests and running wild, yet he influenced President Roosevelt in 1903 to protect Yosemite in California: he gave not just the US but the world the concept of the national park. His inspiration came home to Scotland, engaging people in the preservation of places like Knoydart, Assynt and Schiehallion. Muir saw the world shrinking and found a voice that made a difference. He was not alone; other 19th century writers understood the connections in the web of life and saw how they were being severed. Edward Green Balfour, a Scottish surgeon who served in India from the 1830s was, for example, one of the first people to sound warnings about the damaging effects of deforestation on watercourses, thus acting as a catalyst of famine. A hero amongst foresters, few others remember his name today.

Whilst many writers of prose and poetry have captured the beauty, and sometimes the ferocity, of nature, I consider that two stand out as natural philosophers of great distinction. From completely different backgrounds and through very different life experiences, Patrick Geddes (a Scots biologist and town planner, 1854 – 1932) and Aldo Leopold (an American ecologist, forester and environmentalist, 1887 – 1948) both looked closely at the world around them, saw how it worked and translated their observations into manifestos for social change. Leopold's Land Ethic and Geddes' concept of the Valley Section provide two quite different but highly compatible ways of thinking about the relationship between people and nature in general and about the particular ways in which we derive livelihoods through the use of natural resources. In 1948 Aldo Leopold wrote: "A land ethic, then, reflects the existence

**Below**: "Of all the mountain ranges I have climbed, I like the Sierra Nevada best", wrote John Muir (right) seen here with President Theodore Roosevelt at Glacier Point, Yosemite in 1903. Image: courtesy of US National Park Service.

of an ecological conscience, and this in turn reflects a conviction of individual responsibility for the health of land." (We will return to the issue of responsibility later in this book.) In the space age, Leopold's insightful observation that, "The landscape of any farm is the owner's portrait of himself" lends itself to expansion. A moon-based observer might well remark that the landscape of Earth is humankind's portrait of itself. And it was Leopold, commenting on our meddling impact on nature, who taught us that, "The first rule of intelligent tinkering is to keep all the pieces". Patrick Geddes is often summed up by his phrase "By leaves we live". Those four sparse words capture the way the world works. It took him only four more to tell us what to do about it: "Think global, act local" (from *Cities in Evolution,* published in 1915). Between them, Muir, Leopold and Geddes would have known how to run a small planet, yet their prescience and wisdom has largely passed us by.

## One small step

It may have been, as many people have suggested, the view of the Earth from space that began to stir us. Seeing the whole world for the first time, we realised how small it is. I

**Facing page**: Giant redwoods in the John Muir Grove, Royal Botanic Garden Edinburgh. Image: RBGE/ Lynsey Wilson.

**Below**: "There are some who can live without wild things, and some who cannot" wrote Aldo Leopold, shown here indicating the growth in a planted red pine (*Pinus resinosa*) in 1946. Image: courtesy of the Aldo Leopold Foundation Archives. Photograph by Robert A. McCabe.

# A river of timber

*A travelling botanist is witness to some of the most hapless accidents our species can devise. I remember a conversation with a former colleague at the Natural History Museum in London, just back from a plant collecting expedition to Borneo. Enviously I asked how it had been. He looked at me like an extra from* Apocalypse Now *and said, "We travelled up river for three days. We didn't see water, we just saw a river of timber. There was no forest on the riverbank, it had all been clear-felled. We got to the forest in the end, but I am never going back. I couldn't bear to see that again." I felt numb. I would have preferred to continue the waking dream that Borneo was a paradise for botanists – an unbroken forest shaped by nature and untouched by man. My colleague had a faraway look and I knew he was still in shock. Post Traumatic Shock is not generally associated with botanists who have been to planet Earth's remote places and its glorious rainforests. But too often now those who have been bear the scars.*

Honduras 1992: having collected herbarium specimens in Olancho Province, many from recently felled trees, we returned to our base amongst a succession of lorries carrying a depressingly different cargo from the same source. Image: Stephen Blackmore.

## Think global, act local

Few people could name the person who gave us the rallying cry of environmentalism and sustainable development. Patrick Geddes is not easy to pigeonhole. He was a biologist, educator, city planner, gardener and, above all, philosopher and visual thinker who made complex concepts manageable and systematic.

Born in Ballater, Scotland, in 1854, he grew up in Kinnoul and amongst other positions held the Chair of Botany at University College, Dundee, from 1888 to 1919. Geddes promoted not the three Rs of traditional education but the three Hs: heart, hand and head, arguing that instinct and feeling (heart) should be followed by practical exploration (hand) leading to abstraction (head). His image of the Valley Section related the general slope from mountain to sea with the occupations of the inhabitants from countryside to city. It captures a deep understanding of the evolution of landscape and its human occupation. He developed a format of squared or folded paper to capture ideas in a "thinking machine" and gave us such

phrases as "By leaves we live" and "Vivendo discimus" (By living we learn). He was knighted in 1932, the year of his death, and although his legacy lives on he is the classic example of the prophet not widely recognised in his own land.

| MINER | WOODMAN | HUNTER | SHEPHERD | PEASANT | GARDENER | FISHER |

**Top**: Sketch of Patrick Geddes by Etta J. Johnston for *College Magazine* in 1889. Image: courtesy of University of Dundee Archive Services.

**Right**: A drawing showing Geddes' Valley Section. Illustration: Redrawn by Sarah Batey.

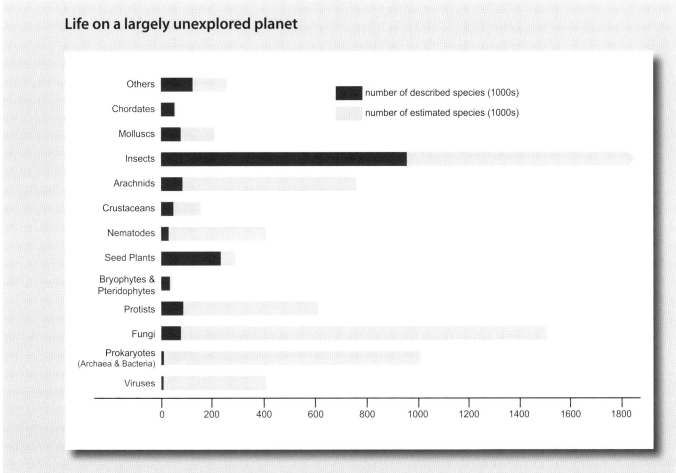

## Life on a largely unexplored planet

- number of described species (1000s)
- number of estimated species (1000s)

For most major groups of organisms the estimated number of species greatly exceeds the number so far described. For insects it is literally off the chart. Source: UK Systematics Forum.

Graph: Redrawn by Sarah Batey.

remember staying up late one night in 1969 to watch Apollo 11 land on the moon and even photographed the 'small step for mankind' as it happened on black and white television. It seemed then that our species had come of age and was poised to reach for the stars. Since then we have indeed looked into deepest space and we can detect planets with some of the characteristics that suggest they might be suitable for life. But still, as always when we look towards the heavens, we are looking out from the only planet that we know with certainty has life.

And what a super-abundance of life the Earth has. An estimated 13 million species share the planet although so far we have only noticed and named about 1.7 million of them. It is a sobering thought that over one million of

them are insects. A few are mammals like us. Of the world's 4,600 species of mammals, 40% are considered by the World Conservation Union (IUCN) to be threatened with extinction. Almost half our closest relatives are struggling for their very survival yet we have still to meet most of our other neighbours. A highly readable account of why this is so can be found in Edward O. Wilson's book *The Diversity of Life* (1992). It may seem surprising or at least a little neglectful that we do not know precisely how many species we share the planet with. On a world with no new continents, where are they hiding, these millions of unknown species? Most, Wilson explains, are microscopic, too small to be seen by the naked eye. Many are in places we have scarcely explored, the deep oceans that

**Above**: Mankind's mark on the moon: the only place in the universe, apart from Earth, that bears the footprint of any living thing (as far as we know). Image: courtesy of NASA/JSC scan.

**Opposite**: Aboriginal rock painting depicting a hunter and a kangaroo, from Kakadu National Park.
Image:
© iStockphoto.com/zbindere. Reproduced with kind permission of Kakadu National Park and its staff.

cover two thirds of our planet, the rainforest canopy and even the soil beneath our feet. We only know they exist by projecting forward from the numbers of new species described each year across all groups of organisms.

The certainty that we are one of at least 1.7 million species that have evolved here on Earth excites me much more than the possibility, much though I long for it, that there are other living worlds in the universe. Worlds with life that would seem even more impossible to us than the duckbilled platypus first encountered by Europeans in 1798. When a pelt was sent to London by the Governor of New South Wales it was thought to be a hoax!

It is fun to imagine sailing through space to one of these worlds in a cabin as cramped as Joseph Banks' quarters on the *Endeavour*. What an adventure that would be! But I remain happier continuing to travel this beautiful Earth, where we know beyond doubt that, for now, life is abundant and thriving and so it will continue if we come to understand the global garden.

### The supreme goddess

Perhaps what has caused us to stir in our sleep is closer to home than the view of Earth from space. James Lovelock's inspirational book *Gaia: A New Look at Life on Earth* published in 1979 was a monumental milestone. Gaia, the living earth in which all is connected like a single organism, strikes me as one of the biggest, most astonishing and most poetic ideas ever conceived by a human mind. So big, so all-encompassing that a blink of the eye distracts us from it. Yet the Gaia hypothesis puts us firmly in our place and stands as the most profound, the most complete, observation of the human condition. It places humans, inescapably, as part of this planet, whether we like it or not. It reminds us that we can breathe because life on the land became a practical alternative to life in the oceans when the atmosphere became rich enough in oxygen. We abandoned gills in favour of lungs because we evolved on a living planet where plants led the colonisation of land. Later on, our brains got bigger and we swung down from the trees in Africa and began to walk across the surface of what then seemed like an endless world. Sometimes we cut down trees to make boats. One way or another we got everywhere.

So it may just be that a kind of Gaia is deeply rooted in the human consciousness. Similar ideas of a living, interconnected world can be traced back much further in time and in many cultures. The idea of the dreamtime in Aboriginal culture entrances me. Looked at from the 21st century, the dreamtime can seem like any other creation myth, yet so much of it can be accounted for by facts that it is better seen for what it is: a well preserved memory of where we came from in the deep past. A memory of the Australian continent before the climate became drier; when giant wombat and giant kangaroo walked the land.

### The simple act of living

Perhaps we have not been woken by words or images but simply by personal experiences in our own lives as we see the world immediately around us becoming more uniform, less rich than the hedgerows and verges of our childhoods. It is easy to dismiss this as a personal dreamtime, an illusion that everything was richer and finer when we were in our infancy. It can't really have been so, can it? Sadly,

## Ostriches are not so stupid

Despite the evidence, some people are in denial, dismissing climate change, biodiversity loss, pollution and the dwindling supply of fossil fuels. Politicians, they say, see the environment as a means of extracting higher taxes while scientists just want to get more funding for their work. If only they were right with their reassuring responses: "We have been here before. The world can get along fine without us interfering. Nature always sorts itself out. The climate always changes."

It is not so. We have not been here before, even if, in some respects, the planet has. The people who survived the last Ice Ages lived in small, self-sufficient communities. Today's complex global village, inhabited by specialists consuming commodities from around the world, would not survive major environmental changes in recognisable form. Perhaps the world would get along fine without humans. Viewed dispassionately, nature can indeed take care of itself. So, even if there were mass extinctions and our own species disappeared into oblivion, others would survive. Earth would still be the richest living planet in the solar system. It is just that we would no longer be around to appreciate it.

Denial, as a human response to stress, works up to a point, enabling some to survive and our species to continue into the future. But in a world at the crossroads, avoiding reality will, at best, see us survive into a future poorer than today. With our eyes wide open we can do much better than that.

And of course, ostriches do not actually bury their heads in the sand as some humans do: after all, that would just speed up their demise.

Image: © Simon van Noort, Iziko Museums of Cape Town.

as the next chapter demonstrates, the answer is yes. The world of today is very different, and poorer, than the world of my childhood in the 1950s. The landscapes of childhood are still there, more or less, though towns, villages and cities have all spread into the countryside. But looking more closely at lanes and moors that might seem unchanged from space, we find that once-common inhabitants have slipped away. They have not just disappeared around the next bend, they have gone from the whole county if not the entire country.

In the end it doesn't really matter what has brought us out of our dreams. The important thing is that we recognise that the world needs our help rather than our continuing, disinterested plunder. Now that we are awake to the scale of the ecological challenges that confront us, the prospects look terrifying. The global climate is changing and, around the world, nature is on the retreat. This is a depressing reality but we must not allow a sense of hopelessness to overwhelm us. However much has been lost, despair will only delay or dilute our response. The time to come to the aid of our planet is now. The law of diminishing returns dictates that the longer we wait before accepting responsibility and taking action, the less there will be to save. Some people are still in denial, telling themselves that all is well on planet Earth. It is a seductive idea that excuses inaction.

Jared Diamond's *Collapse*, published in 2005, sums up the human predicament. Whether civilisations and societies perish or survive depends on how they choose to live in relation to nature. Some sleepwalk into catastrophe whilst others find a sustainable existence even when the natural resources to hand are limited. The problems we now face are essentially the consequences of using the natural resources of the planet faster than they can replace themselves. We cannot continue to find what we need by going a little further over the next hill. Like the inhabitants of Easter Island who some believe cut down the last trees to create their monolithic statues, we too might find our present way of life ends abruptly, leaving a new way to be found.

The ancient Maya established Caracol in the Chiquibul Forest of Belize in around 300 BC. It became a major force, rivalling Tikal in Guatemala until a sudden decline around 900 AD. The level forest canopy engulfing such ruins makes them difficult to detect from the air. Image: Stephen Blackmore.

# Malawi

*Collecting plants along a dried-up watercourse near Zomba, Malawi in 1979 with my colleague Elias Banda, a village chief came to talk us. He looked thoughtful then explained that people in the village were concerned because the stream no longer flowed all year and life was becoming harder, especially for the women. Firewood as well as water was becoming scarcer. Soon the women would have to go over the hill and into the next valley to cut firewood. Elias and I exchanged anxious glances. Despite the wisdom and traditions of the community there was much the chief could not know when he found himself encountering environmental change driven by the growth of the village. Clearly he was unaware that villagers in adjacent valleys shared the same predicament. Why should he know? It had never been necessary or relevant in the past. Elias explained that our work, searching for plants, took us to many valleys so we had seen that the lower slopes of every valley in the region were bare of trees. "What can we do?" asked the headman. "You must plant trees," Elias replied, "as many trees as you can". Sadly, when I next visited Malawi, after a gap of some 24 years, I saw that many hillsides were completely bare of trees, except for a few kinds that cannot be used for fuel wood, right up to their eroded summits.*

The author on Mulanje Mountain, Malawi. It is not yet certain why the trees of Mulanje cedar *(Widdringtonia whytei)*, in the background, are dying. Image: Elizabeth Blackmore

# CHAPTER 3

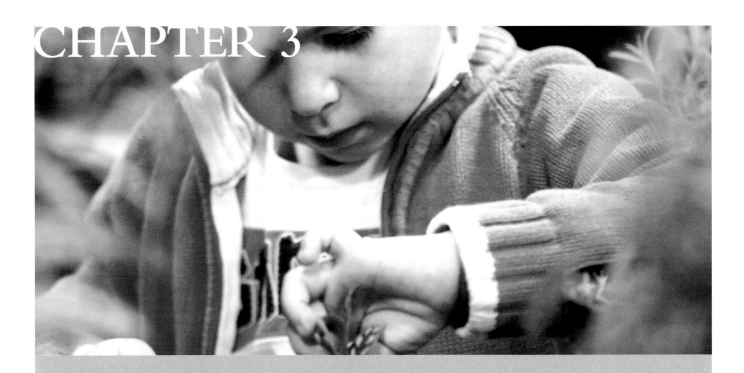

## ALL THESE I LEARNT

"If I have a son, he shall salute the lords and ladies who unfurl green hoods to the March rains, and shall know them afterwards by their scarlet fruit.

He shall know the celandine, and the frigid, sightless flowers of the woods, spurge and spurge laurel, dogs' mercury, wood-sorrel and queer four-leaved herb-paris fit to trim a bonnet with its purple dot.

He shall see the marshes gold with flags and kingcups and find shepherd's purse on a slag-heap...

He shall know the butterflies that suck the brambles, common whites and marbled white, orange-tip, brimstone, and the carnivorous clouded yellows...

All these I learnt when I was a child and each recalls a place or occasion that might otherwise be lost.

They were my own discoveries.

They taught me to look at the world with my own eyes and with attention.

They gave me a first content with the universe.

Town-dwellers lack this intimate content, but my son shall have it!"

From the poem *All these I learnt* by Robert Byron, 1905–41.

*All These I Learnt* by Robert Byron (© Robert Byron) is reproduced by permission of PFD (www.pfd.co.uk) on behalf of The Estate of Robert Byron.

# A SUCCESSION OF ACCIDENTS

Today is important. It started like any other day but after today the world will never be quite the same again because the sun will set on a poorer world. Perhaps we will not even notice and will all just carry on with life as usual. After all, the steady impoverishment of the planet has become normal. It happens every day, whether we are looking or not. It is not something we have decided to do, merely a succession of accidents.

Although the world of nature is slipping away, much remains. The world is still a beautiful place even at the dawn of the sixth great extinction. There are plenty of new species waiting to be discovered and lots of exploration to be done. With maps and without, I have known the excitement of walking through forests of giant trees in the rainforests of Honduras and Sulawesi and climbing above the tree line in the Himalayas. I have lived on an atoll, just above sea level, where the vegetation is grazed and dominated by giant tortoises with flightless land birds following in their wake. For me, the fact that satellite images show every tree on the Jade Dragon Snow Mountain in Yunnan Province, China, enhances rather than

**Facing page**: Discovering the world through a child's eyes. Image: courtesy of Eamonn McGoldrick.

**Below**: The Aldabran flightless rail (*Dryolimnas cuvieri aldabranus*), the last surviving flightless bird of the Indian Ocean. Image: Stephen Blackmore.

**Above:** When the Chalillo Dam was commissioned in 2005 it flooded a thousand hectares of riverside forest, displacing tapirs, jaguars, scarlet macaws and other threatened species from their best stronghold in the Maya Mountains of Belize. Image: Stephen Blackmore.

diminishes the joy of being there. But too often there has been a bitter edge to these experiences of nature, a sense of our precious biological heritage slipping away. Once it was seeing and hearing mahogany trees falling to chain saws in a remote province of Honduras. Another time it was flying in a military helicopter over the construction site of an ill-conceived dam that has since flooded one of the finest forests in Belize. More often, it is simply looking in the right places for once-common wildflowers, birds or butterflies, and failing to find them.

## Our disappearing world

Much of our natural heritage, the biological richness of our world, has already been lost and yet more species will follow into oblivion unless we respond urgently. This matters because climate change cannot be separated from the loss of biodiversity. The world is connected and it needs the property of the richness of life, or biodiversity, if it is to continue to work as we expect it to.

This diversity flows continuously through all life on Earth: from the individual to the species to the ecosystem. The genetic diversity between individuals endows them with different characteristics and these shape interactions in nature. One school of thought tries to understand the ecology of the world in terms of functional species, each of which performs set tasks like a cog in a machine. How many species cogs do we need for the world to keep turning? No one knows, so let's assume it is all of them. The idea of functional species is a useful abstraction but should not be confused with reality. All trees are not equal: the juniper hugs the ground on windswept mountainsides where pine cannot stand; beech favours well-drained slopes; alder likes its feet in water. No two species are the same and none stands alone, each interacts with others higher or lower in the food chain.

Who is to say which species are important? Best not to try, they are all linked together in the complex web of life in which every human being is also a strand. This complexity is now disappearing as a side effect of our demands on the planet. Some species we have hunted or harvested to extinction, others have been starved of prey, but most that have become extinct did so when their habitat was destroyed. When we hear of habitat loss, an image of a far-off tropical rainforest falling before the chainsaw may spring to mind but it is also close to home in the disappearance of hedgerows, the draining of bogs and meadows or the conquest of urban landscapes by concrete.

**Below:** It is possible to hint at the myriad of interactions between living things in Scotland which has lost its top predators and much of its temperate forest. Imagine how difficult it is to capture the complexity of the web of life in a tropical forest or coral reef. Illustration: Sarah Batey.

## The web of life

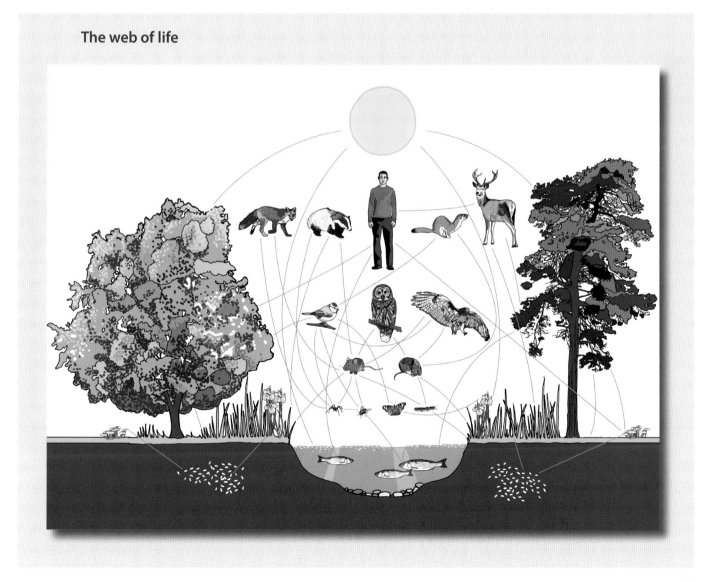

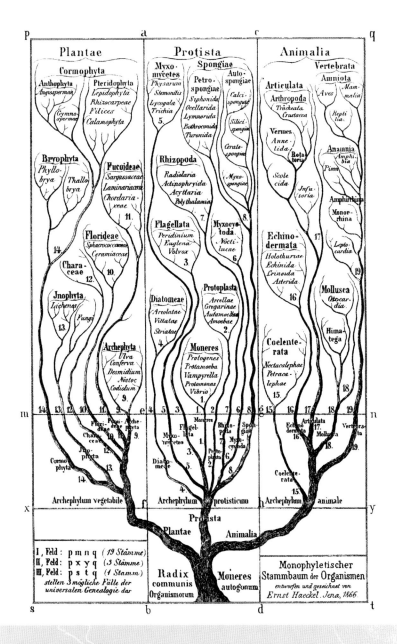

## The tree of life

The evolutionary branching and diversification of life on Earth from a "common root" was represented, quite literally, as a tree (above) by Ernst Haeckel in 1866. Simple life forms that could harness the energy of the sun through the process of photosynthesis originated around 3 billion years ago, near the base of the tree. As they evolved into increasingly complex algae and later into land plants the process of photosynthesis became the principal source of energy for an ever greater diversity of animals. As living things became more diverse, through these vast periods of time, so the number of interactions between them grew, becoming ever more complex and interwoven. This is how the web of life, of which we are part, was assembled.

**Above:** Ernst Haeckel's 'Monophyletic tree of organisms' first published in *Generelle Morphologie der Organismen, 1866.*.

## Crisis, what crisis?

The global human population has doubled twice in the last century and now stands at more than 6.6 billion. Ways of life that might have been sustainable for centuries when practised on a smaller scale cannot simply be scaled up because nature does not have the capacity to support them. Perhaps it could be argued that the extinction of a few rare species might scarcely be noticed, but the scale of the biodiversity crisis threatens to turn extensive areas of land and sea into deserts or barren wastes. This inevitably leads to the breakdown of the ecosystem services on which we, and all other living things, depend.

Thus when we speak of the biodiversity crisis we refer to the accelerating erosion of the diversity of life at the level of the genetically distinct individual, the species and the ecosystem. The ultimate expression of biodiversity loss is extinction, the irreversible snuffing out of a distinct kind of life. Once living things have gone, they cannot be brought back. There may be little need to mourn life forms like the dinosaurs that are long gone. But we are the poorer for the loss of any species that might still exist if they had not encountered humanity: we are all pieces of the same jigsaw puzzle.

It's easy to forget more recent losses: the passenger pigeon, which went from common to extinct in a few decades, disappearing forever in 1914; the flightless great auk, eaten to extinction by the 1850s. It took us a century to eat the most famous flightless bird, the dodo, to extinction in the mid 17th century, but a mere 30 years to consume Steller's sea cow after its discovery in the 18th century. They and hundreds of other species are gone and largely forgotten.

What about the present extinction crisis? It is certain that many species will become extinct and that will make the world a poorer place. But there is an even more invidious component to the crisis: the biological impoverishment of our planet. This may not quite involve complete extinction, but means that large numbers of species become very rare, teetering on the brink. A world in which many species survive only by clinging on to life in a few remote reserves is not a healthy, green,

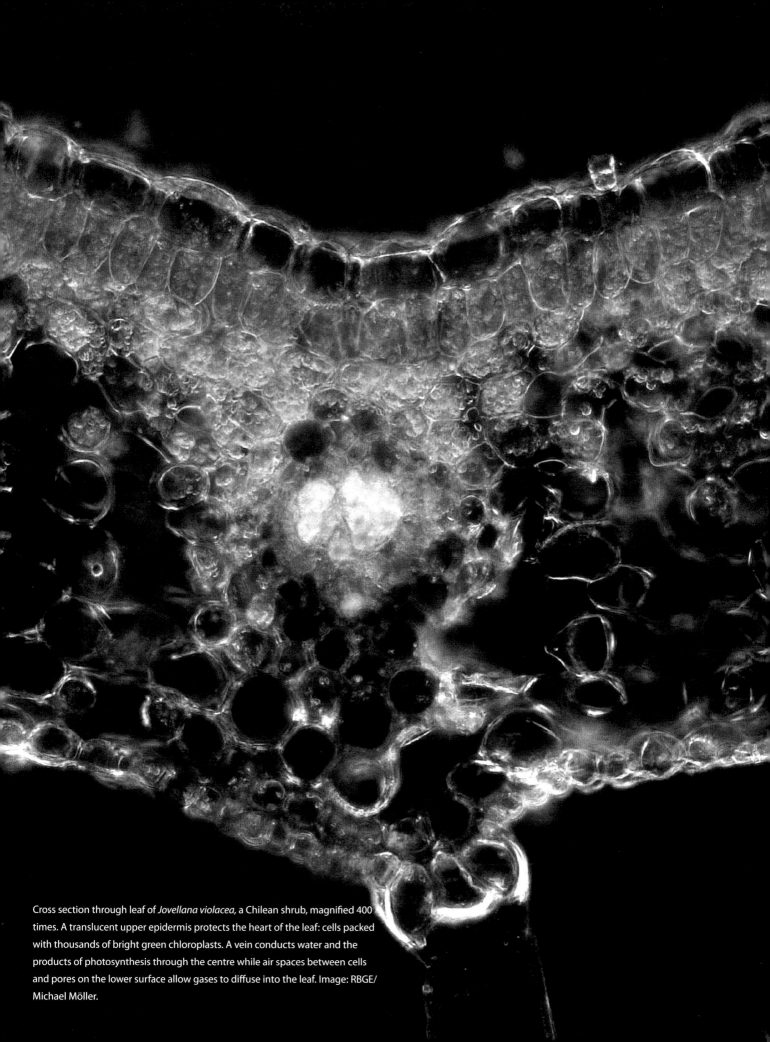

Cross section through leaf of *Jovellana violacea,* a Chilean shrub, magnified 400 times. A translucent upper epidermis protects the heart of the leaf: cells packed with thousands of bright green chloroplasts. A vein conducts water and the products of photosynthesis through the centre while air spaces between cells and pores on the lower surface allow gases to diffuse into the leaf. Image: RBGE/ Michael Möller.

## Defining biodiversity

Biodiversity, short for biological diversity, has its own United Nations Convention. According to the Convention, "Biological diversity means the variability among living organisms from all sources including, *inter alia*, terrestrial, marine and other aquatic ecosystems and the ecological complexes of which they are part; this includes diversity within species, between species and of ecosystems."
More simply, biodiversity essentially refers to the diversity of all life, everywhere on Earth and at every level, from the ecosystem to the genetically distinct individual.

The United Nations Convention on Biological Diversity (CBD) was established at the 1992 Earth Summit in Rio De Janeiro, not just because of the threats to nature but also as an attempt to establish a more equitable sharing of benefits accruing from nature as a source of useful new genes or species. The work of the Convention is examined more closely in Part Two.

**Above**: The great auk *(Pinguinus impennis)*, a flightless seabird with no fear of humans, was hunted for food, eggs and down. The last one in Britain was killed on St Kilda in July 1840. Image: © The Natural History Museum, London.

living planet. For someone born in the 1950s it is easy to see how the biological impoverishment of the British Isles has progressed, with once-common and familiar wildflowers, birds and butterflies becoming increasingly scarce. Plantlife, the excellent conservation organisation that champions plants when animals dominate the limelight, estimates that every year in the British Isles a native plant species becomes locally extinct. One might think that only global extinction matters. Should we care about losing a species in the British Isles if it is widespread in Europe?

Yes, because local populations may well be genetically distinct from those in other places and therefore possess the ability to thrive under slightly or even significantly different conditions. For example, genetic diversity is high among wild Scottish salmon because their offspring return to the same river to breed. This local adaptation accumulated over thousands of generations becomes increasingly distinct and all the more vulnerable if young fry are introduced from different watercourses. Similarly, the Scots pine (*Pinus sylvestris* variety *sylvestris*) differs from trees of the same species elsewhere in Europe and can grow in distinctly wetter conditions.

## Competing for space and food

We rightly find it startling that some of the Earth's most spectacular inhabitants – tigers, giant pandas, rhinoceroses and now even polar bears – are facing extinction in the wild. It is right to be shocked, but an even stronger reaction is called for when we consider the very much larger number of smaller, less charismatic species now so rare that their status is uncertain. We hope they are still out there, somewhere, but with the exception of large animals, the passing of the last of a kind is rarely witnessed.

Habitat loss is the over-riding factor driving the impoverishment of nature. Competition for space is so intense that many species will have nowhere to live. Each of the wonderful animals we are so concerned about is connected through the web of life with other species which it depends upon for food. Often those species are themselves threatened. Tigers and polar bears, in common with other top predators, are at the top of the food chain, like us. They are threatened with extinction not simply because the animals they hunt are vanishing but because their habitat is disappearing leaving them without the living space or prey they need. Tigers face an additional threat because they are believed to have medicinal properties that make them worth more dead than alive. Pandas and rhinos are herbivorous, getting their energy directly from the plants they eat. For them too, a green planet with natural vegetation is the key to the future, providing that a human fondness for animal parts, including rhino horns, can be curbed.

Human interest tends to focus on the large and charismatic animals sharing the planet. But it is important to remember that plants are at the base of the global food chains, key strands in the web of life and essential for the survival of large animals including us. Just as tigers and rhinos are pursued for their alleged powers, so those plants that have medicinal uses are also facing over-harvesting in the wild.

**Below**: Pressure from grazing animals, especially red deer, has halted natural regeneration of trees in many parts of Scotland. Once fences keep the deer out saplings rapidly spring up from the soil seed bank as here in the Cairngorms National Park. Image: Stephen Blackmore.

## No longer common or garden

Many familiar species are in decline, even if they are not yet facing extinction:

- The house sparrow *(Passer domesticus)* is in sharp decline in the UK together with the starling *(Sturnus vulgaris)* and song thrush *(Turdus philomelos)*.
- Oxlip *(Primula elatior)*, Scottish dock *(Rumex aquaticus)* and other wildflowers of wet places.
- Victims of collecting crazes like holly fern *(Polystichum lonchitis)*.
- Victims of introduced diseases such as the wych elm *(Ulmus glabra)* and Dutch elm disease.
- Cornflower *(Centaurea cyanus)* and other arable weeds have declined because of modern farming techniques.

## Alien invaders

Biodiversity is also under pressure because humans have a habit of moving species around the globe, either intentionally because they might be useful or unintentionally as stowaways. Sometimes conditions at the end of the journey are unfavourable and numbers of introduced species remain low. But sometimes the incomers find conditions better than at home, either because they have escaped from natural enemies or they find an abundance of places that meet their preferences. Once invading species get a toehold they often compete so aggressively with native species that they crowd out the original inhabitants.

Climate change heightens the risk of invading species taking hold. As conditions at high latitude become milder, species begin to arrive that would have not have survived in the harsher conditions of the past. Nature is very finely tuned. Humans can scarcely detect a difference of half a degree centigrade but that can be sufficient for new pests and diseases, in particular, to extend their range.

Invasive species in the British Isles have been relatively few in number. This is not to say that the release of mink or grey squirrels has not had disastrous consequences for native mammals such as otters and red squirrels. And amongst invasive plants, *Rhododendron ponticum*, Japanese knotweed (*Fallopia japonica*), giant hogweed (*Heracleum mantegazzianum*) and Himalayan balsam (*Impatiens glandulifera*) have done a vast amount of expensive damage. All are escaped plants introduced in British gardens for ornamental purposes, several of them in the early decades of the 19th century. Despite the serious threat they pose to native plants, they represent a relatively mild example of what invasive plants and animals can do. Rabbits and cane toads in Australia have done greater damage. The extensive grasslands of California are now almost entirely composed of species introduced from Europe. Numerous attempts to improve the grazing has displaced less competitive prairie natives.

## The real economy of the planet

Photosynthesis powers our planet, on land and in the oceans, generating the oxygen we breathe and the food we eat. In the marine world the most significant contributors are algae, including unicellular algae that occur in vast numbers as plankton, forming the base of marine food chains. On land it is the forests of the world that are the most productive ecosystems.

Humankind has taken forests for granted over millennia but fortunately huge tracts of the world are still forested. What matters now

Facing page, clockwise from **top:** House sparrow (*Passer domesticus*). Image: Sue Tranter (rspb-images.com); Oxlip (*Primula elatior*). Image: RBGE archives; Holly fern (*Polystichum lonchitis*). Image: RBGE/Heather McHaffie; Scottish dock (*Rumex aquaticus*). Image: RBGE/Debbie White; Dutch elm disease on wych elm (*Ulmus glabra*). Image: RBGE/Max Coleman; Cornflower (*Centaurea cyanus*). Image: RBGE/Heather McHaffie.

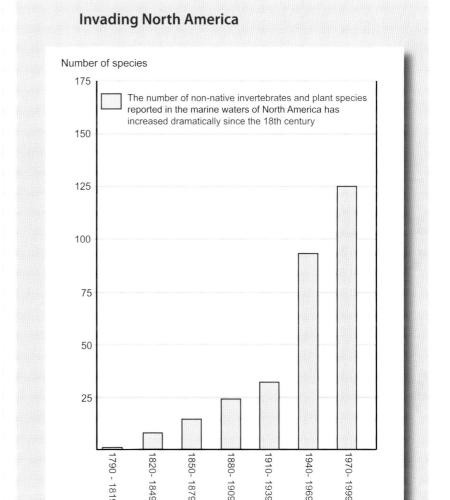

### Invading North America

Number of species

The number of non-native invertebrates and plant species reported in the marine waters of North America has increased dramatically since the 18th century

Image: courtesy of Millennium Ecosystem Assessment. Adapted from figures used in the MA synthesis reports originally prepared by Philippe Rekacewicz and Emmanuelle Bournay of UNEP/Grid-Arendal. Tables in the synthesis reports were created by Dever Designs.

# Dancing with wolves

*There are remnants of European vegetation that survived the Industrial Revolution and are little changed since the end of the Ice Ages. In 1992 I visited the Bialowieza National Park in eastern Poland, the last extensive example of a high-canopied European broadleaf forest. Speeding under towering oak trees on a horse-drawn sledge through the forest in winter, knowing that wolves still ran in the forest, I felt like a figure in a folk story.* Peter and the Wolf *perhaps.*

*In this ancient forest, brown bear (Ursus arctos), wild boar (Sus scrofa), European bison (Bison bonasus) and a handful of European lynx (Lynx lynx) still survive. These animals — eliminated across most of the rest of Europe because of their threat, more perceived than real, to human interests — survive here for two simple reasons. First, because of the plants: large mammals need a reasonably large and undisturbed habitat in which to live. Second, because of people: the forest was protected as a royal hunting ground where animals prospered. Thus it was saved from being opened for farmland. To walk in such a forest in Europe in the 21st century is a rare privilege.*

The horse-drawn sledge I travelled in through the Bialowieza National Park, Poland.

Image: Stephen Blackmore.

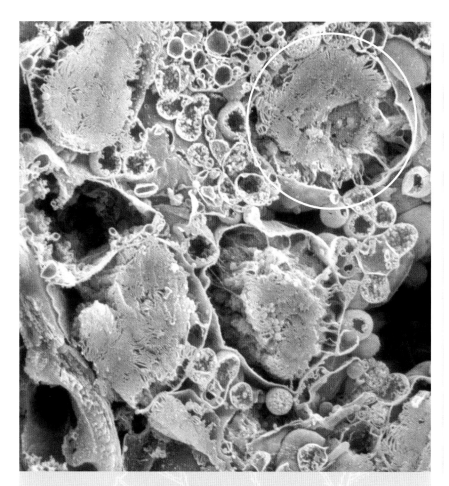

## The leaf factory provides the air we breathe

Like sunbathers, leaves present the maximum surface area to the sky to soak up energy from the sun's rays. Standing beneath a beech tree looking upwards, you will appreciate how the spreading branches position the leaves to catch as much light as possible. Looking within a leaf reveals further sophistication: elongated cells, like fibre optics, convey light through to the centre where each cell contains numerous green chloroplasts, (like the one circled above in a freeze-fractured leaf cell magnified 4,000 times): the microscopic structures where photosynthesis takes place. These too have found a way of exposing the maximum surface area to the sunlight. Each chloroplast contains stacked sheets of membranes perfectly aligned for the capture of light where solar energy is converted to chemical energy. On its lower surface the leaf has closable pores that regulate the loss of water vapour and the flow of atmospheric gases.

It was the leaf factory that created our breathable atmosphere, adding oxygen over millions of years. Only when the atmosphere was rich enough in oxygen needed to release energy by burning food could life emerge onto land. Overall, for the last one and a half billion years, photosynthesis caused carbon dioxide levels in the atmosphere to fall. The balance of carbon dioxide and oxygen has varied greatly through time but since the Industrial Revolution there has been a significant and accelerating increase in atmospheric carbon dioxide, causing the greenhouse effect.

Image: Stephen Blackmore.

and for the future is that we come to understand the part forests play in maintaining life on Earth (their protection and expansion are some of the most immediate and effective responses to climate change, as we shall see later). Their role in the life of the planet is fundamental. Just as a human can survive with a single lung, so can planet Earth. We should not, however, expect it to run a marathon and yet that is what we are demanding by making the assumption that it is fine to continue consuming faster than nature can replenish. While the world's forests refresh the air we breathe, they are also estimated to store 283 gigatons (a gigaton is a billion tons) of carbon in their biomass. It is an astonishing fact that all the carbon locked up in forests – deadwood, leaf litter and soil – exceeds the total amount present in the atmosphere.

This is the real economy of the planet. If we humans consume, directly or indirectly, the products of photosynthesis faster than plants can replace them, then bankruptcy is inevitable. Bill Clinton was right when he said, "It's the economy, stupid," in his successful campaign for the Presidency of the United States in 1992. But, as political leaders generally do, he was distinguishing between the monetary economy of human affairs and the truly planetary economy underpinned by photosynthesis. And no such distinction exists.

Harvesting or logging of old growth forests is the biggest mistake we are making, it is like keeping warm around a fire made of Old Masters. We can translate the cost of this behaviour into the currency of the monetary economy and a recent European Commission report entitled *The Economics of Ecosystems and Biodiversity* has done just that, concluding that deforestation around the world costs us the equivalent of about 6% of Gross Domestic Product (GDP) every year.

### System failures

A further alarming dimension to biodiversity loss is the failure of ecosystem services. Just one example: in a tropical rainforest we might come upon a smouldering clearing where trees have been felled and their remains torched. The land is being opened up to make space for new

crops. Next year, citrus trees will be planted to meet international demand for a glass of juice to start the day. But even before the citrus arrives, heavy tropical rain begins to wash away the thin organic layer of soil. Rivers now run heavy with sediment as the land is stripped of the very soil the new crops require. Cleared of forest, water runs swiftly into the rivers rather than percolating slowly and steadily. With no tree cover, the soil may be next to go. Soon streams and tributaries begin to dry up, flowing only when heavy rain falls. When water ceases to flow, life becomes hard.

Forests in the headwaters of the world's great river systems have a double value as carbon sinks and water sources. Again, climate change compounds challenges. Many of the great rivers run with melt water of glaciers, built up from an excess of winter snow. Glaciers are retreating around the world, especially at lower latitudes nearer to the equator. Without water and with less and less soil, life becomes harder to sustain. The ultimate expression of biodiversity loss is grinding poverty and a miserable existence for humans. When world leaders commit

themselves to the eradication of poverty they need to remember the leaf colony. Only in a healthy, green living world can people prosper.

As if biodiversity and climate change were not enough we have a third major challenge. The human race is over-consuming the world's finite resources of fossil fuels, releasing carbon dioxide and other greenhouse gases into the atmosphere. Reserves of coal are vast and even those of oil and gas are substantial. But our present ways of burning them have appalling side-effects. Not using fossil fuels is one of the best ways of keeping carbon locked up and avoiding global warming. Until relatively recently the main downside of, for example, petrol engines was thought to be the pollution they caused. Having now made the connection between greenhouse gases and global warming, we understand that exhaust fumes have potentially more damaging components than particulates or lead. Not only is the supply of fossil fuels finite unlike many other natural resources – they are also non-renewable. Once they have been consumed they will have gone the way of the dinosaurs. A wiser user of

**Above**: Tropical forest in Belize cleared to plant orange trees for juice. Image: Stephen Blackmore.

oil would conserve it as the only source of chemical components for plastics, lubricants, waxes and hundreds of other products useful in daily life.

How many species can be lost before systems and interactions break down? No one knows, but in many places around the world we are busy performing unintentional experiments that will find out. If nothing else, the precautionary principle suggests that we should strive to "keep all the pieces" as Aldo Leopold suggested. Even the smallest piece could play a vital part. Scientists often contrast the complexity of the web of life with the relative simplicity of even the most sophisticated man-made construction. I am struck by our apparent indifference to the loss of biodiversity in contrast to the extreme concern we would feel on seeing a nut or bolt drop off an aeroplane we are about to travel in. We would be worried by a missing component of an aircraft because we can imagine the catastrophic results its loss might lead to. Compared to the complexity of nature, the aircraft is quite simple.

In summary, humankind's relationship with the planet has become unsustainable. Our relentless removal of forest cover and ravenous appetite for fossil fuels have increased greenhouse gases. The planet is warming beyond the scope of natural climate variation. Whether we accept this is the result of human activities or not, the consequences are inescapable. Today we can look at our world and see that it is still good. But the actions we choose to take in the next five to ten years will define the kind of planet we leave to our children. We stand at a crossroads, or perhaps more accurately a sprawling 'spaghetti junction' offering a confusion of different directions. Which route to take? Before returning to these choices at the end of the book, Part Two explores how botanic gardens are working to help keep life on Earth complex and interwoven.

**Below**: In a complex and fast changing world, how do we decide which route to take? Image: Birmingham Picture Library.

**Facing page**: Running red: a satellite view shows Madagascan rivers carrying topsoil from deforested land. Image: courtesy of NASA's Earth Observatory.

# PART 2:
## WHAT CAN BE DONE?

Botanical research in the field is now a race against time: a sense of urgency drives the global collaboration dedicated to recording, conserving and studying the great wealth of plants on Earth. Here RBGE and Indonesian botanists collaborate at Air Panas, Sumatra. Image: RBGE/Peter Wilkie.

# CHAPTER 4

## PINNING A VALUE TO PLANTS

As foods and medicines, plants are mainstays of the global economy. Just three species – maize, rice and wheat – provide over 40% of the world's food calories. Roughly 80% of our medicines are derived from plants. Yet the majority of plant species have not been assessed to determine whether they have direct medicinal properties or contain molecules that could be synthesised to create medicines.

World trade in ginseng *(Panax ginseng)* exceeds US $50 million per annum. Substances in the ginkgo tree *(Ginkgo biloba)* – found to be effective against cardiovascular diseases – now account for a yearly turnover of US $360 million.

These sums fade into insignificance when compared to the full value of plants as the primary producers at the base of the food chain and the providers of ecosystem services.

Many of our most popular medicinal plants are now threatened by habitat loss or over-harvesting. Amongst the 30% of plant species facing extinction around the world, thousands must be potentially useful to humans. Who do they belong to and what price should we put on them?

# WHO OWNS THE EARTH?

The gardener accepts responsibility for their garden. They might draft in other pairs of hands but they know that if they do not sow the seeds, plant the bulbs, mow the grass or do the weeding then nobody else will. If they do not look after the garden it will soon become choked with weeds and many of the finer plants will be lost. In gardening, ownership and responsibility usually go together. Can taking responsibility for the whole planet be thought of in the same way? I believe it can, if we apply the mindset of the gardener to the challenge. But this requires humans to act as responsible owners of the planet despite the fact that we do *not* own it.

So who does the planet belong to? Our species collectively behaves as though it owns the Earth, dividing it into countries and smaller territories within them, right down to the plots of land that some humans are fortunate enough to possess and call home. This division of land might be practical but it fragments responsibility to the level of nation, county, city or village. This has the effect of reducing individual account-ability to our own small patch and ultimately leaves those who have no stake at all without obligations. There have, however, been other ways of looking at ownership of the Earth. The concept was unknown to Native Americans. "One does not sell the land upon which the people walk," as Tashunka Witko, better known as Chief Crazy Horse, said. Equally perceptively, Aldo Leopold wrote, "We abuse land because we regard it as a commodity belonging to us. When we see land as a community to which we belong, we may begin to use it with love and respect." Humankind cannot sell the Earth nor ever own it; we belong to it.

Prior to the introduction of the United Nations Convention on Biological Diversity (CBD) at the Earth Summit in Rio de Janeiro in 1992, biodiversity and nature had generally been regarded as a global commons, existing for the benefit of all. In many regards this was a happy state of affairs. The Convention changed that by treating the ecosystems, species and genes of biodiversity as belonging to the na-tion in which they occur. This legal framework was intended, in principle, to make it possible for countries to register and benefit from the exploitation of their natural resources. The fact that many ecosystems and species, together with the genes they contain, cross international boundaries and could be registered by more than one country would not matter.

In particular the intention was to protect the rights of poorer nations, especially those in the tropics, which might be rich in biodiversity but

**Facing page:** Terraced paddy fields of rice. Image: RBGE/Janette Latta.

**Above:** A 'living fossil': the ginkgo tree (Ginkgo biloba), a species dating back 270 million years, is used medicinally to stimulate blood circulation and enhance memory function. Image: RBGE/ Stephen Blackmore.

**Above**: Like many high alpine plants with medicinal properties, the several species of snow lotus (*Saussurea simpsoniana* pictured) are rapidly disappearing because of over-harvesting from the wild.
Image: RBGE/Mark Watson.

poor in the capacity to develop new products from it. The new products were envisaged as being either novel chemical compounds or genes that could be exploited in the molecular revolution of genetically modified organisms (GMOs). Viewed from today's perspective it seems unfortunate that the CBD regarded the new commercial opportunities that might come from biodiversity as more valuable than the ecosystem services it had been providing for millennia. Placing a value on global ecosystem services provided by nature is difficult. One estimate, provided by ecological economist Robert Costanza and his co-workers at the University of Maryland, was that ecosystem services could be valued at US $16-54 trillion *per annum*. Global gross national product, for comparison, is around US $18 trillion *per annum*.

## An unfulfilled promise

In the early 1990s big biotechnology companies seemed on the verge of great breakthroughs in the application of molecular biology to develop genetically modified organisms. Genes came to be seen as the most valuable parts of nature. Whilst molecular technologies no doubt hold great promise, the world was not then ready for the GMOs it was being offered and public opinion in Europe became resolutely opposed to their introduction. How different might this chapter of history have been if the big companies promoting these technologies had first brought out products that would have been of direct benefit to consumers rather than to their corporate profits? By breaking the traditional rights of farmers to keep and re-sow seed from their own crops, large corporations made their first genetically modified (GM) products unpalatable.

Premature field trials added to public concern about the spread of modified genes into nature and further strengthened resolve against the new molecular technologies. Whilst it is highly unlikely that such genes would cause harm, it is not surprising that a public being assured by the corporations that genes could not spread was alarmed to learn how readily they did. The case of genetically modified

sunflowers in Mexico provided salutary lessons. Pollinating bees spread the genes far more widely than had been anticipated. This should not have been a surprise; there has been virtually no research into the longevity of pollen or the distance travelled by pollinating insects. The full potential of the genetic revolution remains unfulfilled, although it may yet be realised one day, when the technology is better understood and farmers and consumers are likely to benefit from it at least as much as patent holders.

Even before the widespread adoption of GMOs failed to materialise, a frenzy of eager anticipation of the value of genes coloured thinking about nature. Feverish gold-rush mentalities replaced common sense. The language of the day reflected this clearly when the word bioprospecting was coined. Conservation advocates began to speak of the immense value of the Amazon and other rainforests as gene banks of the world. Since the tropical countries were richest in biodiversity, they should

**Above**: Jackfruit *(Artocarpus heterophyllus)* has been cultivated in India for 6,000 years and is widely grown in tropical countries for its heavy crop of fruits. Image: Stephen Blackmore.

## Gene machines

Valuable genes can be found in seemingly unlikely places. In 1969 a new heat-loving bacterium, *Thermus aquaticus*, was isolated from hot springs in Yellowstone National Park. Because this particular bacterium can survive at high temperatures, it proved possible to isolate from it a heat-resistant enzyme that can make multiple copies of a given strand of DNA. This enzyme is called Taq polymerase (Taq is short for *Thermus aquaticus*) and is now routinely used in molecular biology laboratories in the Polymerase Chain Reaction (PCR) technique made famous in the film *Jurassic Park*.

It is highly unlikely that strands of dinosaur DNA from a fossilised insect could ever be extracted and multiplied but there are many applications in which it is useful to make millions of copies of a particular short segment of DNA. PCR machines or thermocyclers, which look like small kitchen worktop appliances, do this by cycling through a series of precise temperatures. When an extracted sample is first heated the two strands of the DNA helix separate, next Taq polymerase builds two new strands of DNA using the originals as a template. The cycle is automatically repeated 30 or 40 times over a few hours, resulting in millions of exact copies of the original DNA segment. The technique is widely used in DNA fingerprinting and sequencing.

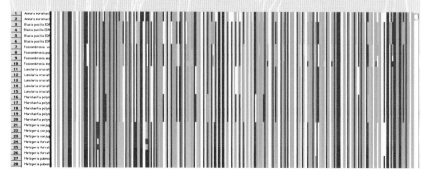

keep their forests for the genetic treasures they contained. Mesmerised by the prospect, many biodiversity-rich countries sought to restrict access to their sovereign biological resources. In practice, there have been few examples of developing nations in the tropics gaining benefits from their biodiversity in this way. For one thing, nature does not recognise international boundaries; distribution of many species transcends national borders. For another, the quest for genes often takes place much closer to home, for example, among sponges and other marine organisms from the European coastline. Since a vast proportion of the genetic inheritance of life is shared, (we humans share 96% of our genes with chimpanzees and 60% with fruit flies) there is less reason than might be imagined to think that the most valuable genes lie in a remote rainforest denizen. This is not to deny that useful genes might not be found in remote places. Many of the most valuable genes for biotechnology have been isolated from extremophiles – those ancient single-celled organisms that evolved in hot springs and deep ocean vents.

Bioprospectors were not just hunting for genes, they also sought novel molecules that would have valuable medicinal properties. These might then be harvested from the plant or animal that produced them or could be chemically synthesised in the laboratory. Just as searching for valuable genes in nature makes sense, so does the quest for novel compounds. Until very recently all of our medicines came from the natural substances found in plants, minerals and animals. So there is every reason to believe that many plant species contain biological compounds that could be immensely valuable as medicines. In many countries, including China and Indonesia, traditional medicines are mainstream. Over 7,000 species of Chinese plants are considered to have medicinal properties including *Artemisia annua*, an invaluable new weapon against malaria, and various species of *Berberis* which provide antibiotics and potential anti-cancer compounds. So bioprospecting was a perfectly valid new twist on one of the ways in which humans have always drawn upon nature. There are doubtless many thousands of valuable natural products awaiting discovery. My concern is that the allure of bioprospecting took our attention away from the even more valuable ecosystem services we find it so easy to overlook.

## The real value of nature

How strange it now seems to have argued that the value of the rainforest was in its genes. How unsurprising that some countries, having been disappointed to find that they could not immediately isolate a cure for cancer or AIDS, should doubt whether it is better to keep a rainforest than to grow soybeans or oil palms. How much better it would have been if the apparently imminent genetic revolution of the early 1990s had never happened and instead the value of rainforests was measured not in their genes but in their ability to create clouds, retain soil, slow the flow of water off the land and soak up carbon dioxide whilst releasing oxygen? How unfortunate that our arrogance urged us to seek short term profits from bio-diversity rather than long term environmental benefits. We can only hope that our species has learnt from these lessons and is emerging from its headlong rush towards the quickest profit, choosing instead a slower and more careful development based on an understanding of the real value of nature: without it we cannot live and prosper.

So despite the fact that, since the Earth Summit in Rio de Janeiro, nature has belonged to nations, there is a strong case for behaving otherwise. It is better to regard the whole planet as belonging to all of us, as a global commons, and to remember that in turn, we belong to it. Our actions now need to transcend the narrow-mindedness of the international convention with which we have bound ourselves. Why? The reason is simply enlightened self-interest. It is in everyone's best interest that we continue to benefit from the natural resources of the planet in ways that do not damage the long-term well-being of ourselves and our fellow citizens.

The concept of sustainable development was devised to encapsulate the idea of using natural resources to support continued economic growth and development without compromising the needs of future generations. It is a wonderful concept but one that we are very

## The economic cost of biodiversity loss

What is the value of biodiversity? The first step towards assessing the world's ecological wealth was taken in Germany in March 2007 when environment ministers of the Group of Eight industrialised countries (Canada, France, Germany, Italy, Japan, Russia, the US and UK) met their counterparts from developing countries (China, India, Brazil, Mexico and South Africa). Together they agreed on what became known as the Potsdam Initiative, a study to evaluate the loss of biodiversity and ecosystems.

Their stated aim: "In a global study we will initiate the process of analysing the global economic benefit of biological diversity, the costs of the loss of biodiversity and the failure to take protective measures versus the costs of effective conservation."

First results from the Interim Report published in 2008 suggest that such a study was long overdue:

• "The well-being of every human population in the world is fundamentally and directly dependent on ecosystem services. However, the levels of many of the benefits we derive from the environment have plunged over the past 50 years as biodiversity has fallen dramatically across the globe."

• "The effect of trends such as these is that approximately 60% of the Earth's ecosystem services that have been examined have been degraded in the last 50 years, with human impacts being the root cause."

• "Applying a 4% discount rate over 50 years implies that we value a future biodiversity or ecosystem benefit to our grandchildren at only one-seventh of the current value that we derive from it!"

Extract from *The Economics of Ecosystems and Biodiversity 2008 (TEEB) Report.*

far from achieving in our present–day relationship with the planet. Even if certain activities are now conducted sustainably, our overall relationship with nature remains predicated on the mistaken notion that more resources are available for our convenience, just over the next horizon. We now live as though there were three Earths, not one.

## Accepting responsibility

Whether we consider ourselves to own it or not, accepting responsibility for the green planet empowers us to act as individuals in tackling today's global challenges. As in our own

**Facing page:** Scientists at work in RBGE's molecular labs (above). A DNA 'barcode' sequence (below). Images: RBGE/Lynsey Wilson (above); RBGE/Michelle Hollingsworth (below).

## Look, it's alive!

"How is the market reacting? What does the market think?" Bull or bear, we endow the global financial markets with living characteristics. The market shapes our lives, whether we are shareholders or not, as we follow its ups and downs, as jobs come and go and fortunes are made and lost. Successes and failures are measured in terms of Gross Domestic Product. But nature, life itself, is treated like a dead thing. We don't ask how it's doing, although to do so would truly gauge our successes and failures. "How is nature reacting? What does nature think?" The fact is it's down! It has been in recession for decades. In this recession, everyone is a shareholder and what is needed now is to invest in nature by tending the global garden.

**Image:** © iStockphoto.com/Artmann Witte.

gardens, we need to accept responsibility for future outcomes. These global challenges are so unprecedented, enormous and overwhelming that it is easy to feel helpless, incapable of making a difference. Individual efforts to discover a more sustainable relationship with the planet seem puny in the face of great uncertainty.

The burden we place upon the planet has increased enormously as the human population has doubled and redoubled. Today the combined actions of 6.6 billion of us, each affecting nature in small ways, adds up to our global problems. Recognising this should enable us to see the other side of the coin: adding up small changes for the better that individuals can make in their daily lives can be sufficient to resolve many of the problems. Depending upon how quickly we act, as individuals and collectively, the benefits that follow will secure a planet for the future that most closely resembles the world of today. I emphasise the contribution of the individual because ultimately it is at the personal level that we must change our relationships with the planet if we are to find a more harmonious and sustainable way forward. This is not to suggest

that governments have no role to play. On the contrary, political leadership is essential, especially in replacing policies that encourage the squander of resources with positive incentives for beneficial outcomes to protect Earth's natural assets. But government action alone will not be enough to avert ecological crisis. Responses that are both necessary and adequate will require leadership by government and action by people. Who leads and who follows? In the end it does not matter, governments and citizens both have many roles to play. Let us not, however, make the mistake we are sometimes inclined to of seeing the problems only too clearly but waiting for 'them' to sort things out. 'They' cannot do it without us.

## Finding a sustainable balance

The fundamental concept of sustainability is using resources in ways that do not prejudice their availability to people in the future. It is often considered to rest upon three pillars: the economy, society and the environment. However, I prefer to visualise these as forces pulling in different directions with sustainability being achieved only when all three are in balance at point ❶ in the figure below. In practice, this has to happen because the monetary economy is widely regarded as more important than the other two forces, pulling us out of balance to point ❷.

It is usually argued that a strong economy is necessary to meet the needs of society, and only once that has been achieved can we afford to look after the environment. Such logic keeps nature on the retreat and the ecological economy in recession. Simple though the idea of sustainability is, it is often difficult to apply in practice. Some resources, like fossil fuels and valuable minerals, are non-renewable and must be eked out if a supply is to be available for future use. Renewable resources such as energy from wind and water, or agricultural produce can be exploited sustainably, provided that a balance is struck. In the case of living resources, the level of renewal needs to exceed the level of consumption, allowing time for nature to recover.

Many traditional forms of agriculture allowed a fallow period or a rotation of crops for the soil to recover and to prevent the build-up of pests. Sustainability was built into the system. Although slash and burn agriculture in the tropics has acquired a bad reputation, it can be perfectly sustainable when there is enough space for it to be practised on a long enough cycle.

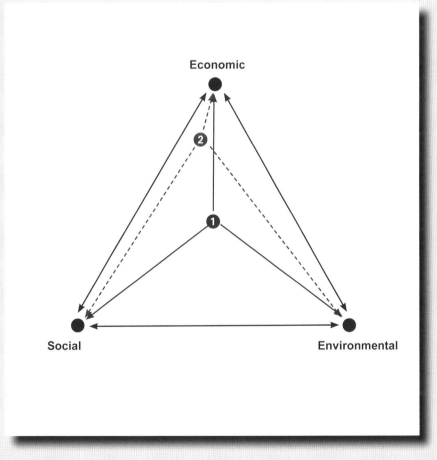

**Illustration: Joanna MacGregor.**

**Next page, clockwise from top**: Broadleaf forest, UK. Image: RBGE/ David Long; mixed conifer forest, China. Image: Stephen Blackmore; swamp forest, Singapore. Image: RBGE/Peter Wilkie; dry forest, Peru. Image: RBGE/Toby Pennington.

## Shared responsibility for Earth's forests

Up to half of Earth's forests, its richest places for life on land, had been cleared before the Industrial Revolution. Despite decades of concern, this assault on the forests has only recently begun to slow down. Even now, 13 million hectares of forest are felled every year. Fortunately, the planet is rich in forests. According to an assessment in 2005 by the Food and Agriculture Organisation (FAO), the world's forests cover just under four billion hectares of which 36% can be regarded as primary forest with little disturbance by humans. This is a fabulous resource of critical importance for its ecosystem services to all, not just the inhabitants of the countries in which primary forest still remains.

Two-thirds of the world's surviving forests are situated in just ten countries: Australia, Brazil, Canada, China, the Democratic Republic of the Congo, India, Indonesia, Peru, the Russian Federation and the United States. These countries, which include some of the largest nations, have a special responsibility for the fate of our naturally forest-covered world. Yet we must all share this burden, because we all use forest products and we all share in the fate of our planet. In huge countries it easy to picture the forest as endless; small countries that have kept their forest are more likely to see the value of what they have.

Belize and Seychelles are two small countries that I am fortunate to know well and both are heavily forested. Both fit our image of tropical paradise and obtain significant income from ecotourism which is just one way of deriving an economic benefit from biodiversity.

# CHAPTER 5

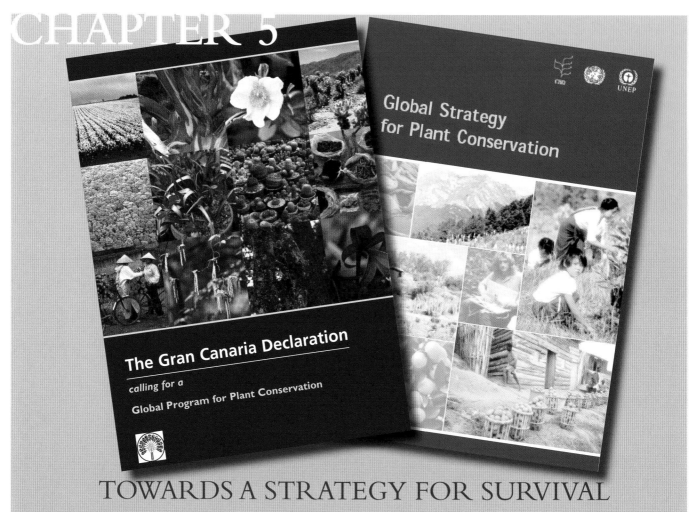

# TOWARDS A STRATEGY FOR SURVIVAL

*"As many as two-thirds of the world's plant species are in danger of extinction in nature during the course of the 21ˢᵗ century, threatened by:*

- *population growth*
- *deforestation*
- *habitat loss*
- *destructive development*
- *over-consumption of resources*
- *the spread of alien invasive species*
- *agricultural expansion.*

*Further loss of plant diversity is predicted through genetic erosion and narrowing of the genetic basis of many species. The disappearance of such vital and massive amounts of biodiversity provides one of the greatest challenges faced by the world community: to halt the destruction of the plant resources that are so essential for present and future needs."*

Extract modified from The Gran Canaria Declaration, 2000.

# A GLOBAL STRATEGY TO SAFEGUARD NATURE

If we agree that we must shoulder responsibility for our planet to ensure a green and healthy global ecosystem, how should we proceed? What practical steps can we take to safeguard nature? Part Three returns to the roles that individuals can play; here I will focus on how botanic gardens are responding to the challenges of protecting plant diversity as the basis of all life on land. First we must consider what to protect, then where and how. There are many opinions on the 'what and where' of conservation but for plants, at least, there is agreement on how they should be protected. The international community has adopted a Global Strategy for Plant Conservation (GSPC) that unites efforts around a set of 16 targets.

## Keeping the web of life woven

What is at risk? All three levels of biodiversity – strands in the web of life – need conserving: the ecosystem, the species and genetic diversity. When we set out to preserve the web of life, we safeguard the complex interactions between species, even those whose existence is as yet unknown. There may be between five and 11 million unknown species on Earth (this estimate is based on the rates at which new ones are being discovered in various groups of organisms and on models of food chains). It is the complexity of nature that delivers the ecosystem services and the range of natural products required to meet our human needs and those of all other species. Preserving the web of life means endeavouring to keep all the pieces of nature intact, thus enabling relationships such as the pollination of flowers by insects or fruit dispersal by birds and mammals to continue. It aims to keep maximum diversity at the levels of ecosystem, species and genetic diversity and, of course, what this means will be different from one place to another.

This matters enormously, although some people are inclined to think that there is much redundancy in the vast diversity of life. In this sense redundancy implies that one tree species, or one ant or bird, is much the same as another. The thinking seems to be that so long as some of them remain (preferably quite a few, but not necessarily all of them) nature will continue to function in familiar ways. Those who take this perspective do accept that not all species are equal. They recognise that some keystone species support so many interactions they are essential to the continued functioning of the ecosystems in which they occur. Fig trees, whose fruits feed a wide range of animals, are often cited as an example. But whilst we can identify some keystone species, a case can also be made for regarding all species as potential keystones. The eminent ecologist Dan Janzen, who has studied the tropical forests of Costa Rica in great detail, points out that often we

**Facing page**: The international community's action plans for global plant conservation. Image: courtesy of Botanic Gardens Conservation International.

**Below**: The bee orchid (*Ophrys apifera*) lives in a mutually beneficial relationship with soil fungi and is pollinated by males of a solitary bee species that mistakes the flowers for their females and attempt to mate. In northern Europe the bee is absent and the bee orchid must rely on self-pollination. Image: RBGE/ Sidney Clarke.

**Above:** Female fig wasps congregate on a Roxburgh's fig *(Ficus auriculata)*. Long whip-like tails inject their eggs inside the developing fruit. Figs are regarded as keystone species in many tropical forests. Image: Stephen Blackmore.

simply do not understand the multiplicity of ways in which species interact. It would be arrogant for us to assume that pieces of nature, whether species, genes or ecosystems, can be lost without making a significant difference.

Those who draw comfort from apparent redundancy in nature are assuming that when one species drops out of the system, another will continue its function. This does happen but we should not let that lull us into the wishful thinking our species is particularly good at. We are, after all, easily misled by simple resemblances and tend to think that one place is very much like another. For example, rainforests the world over generally have a similar physical structure: tall emergent trees towering above a lower canopy of shrubs and saplings spreading

over a ground flora of herbaceous plants. This structural similarity does indeed reflect some general functional similarities, but comparing rainforests in different regions, we find that the species of plants and animals can differ greatly.

Each continent has a different sample of biodiversity, reflecting the complex geological history and movements of the continental plates. In each particular mix, the myriad of interactions between species is critical. Although wind-pollinated plants can live perfectly happily without animal interactions, most tropical rainforest trees depend on animals for pollination or seed dispersal. Dan Janzen uses an eerily accurate label "the living dead" to refer to species of trees whose essential animal partners are extinct. The trees may stand for decades or even centuries more, but they can no longer reproduce unless introduced animal species happen to provide a substitute service. Fortunately this does happen in some cases. In Central and South America, the horse is an effective seed disperser standing in for large, extinct herbivores like the giant sloth.

So there is some redundancy in nature but that does not let us off the hook. Some very widely distributed and distinctive-looking kinds of plants, such as palms, might be thought to be interchangeable in some way because they might all fit into the web of life in more or less the same way. But in fact particular species of palms exhibit considerably different adaptations to fire, floods and interactions with animal species. All six palm species found in the Seychelles islands, for example, belong to different genera, none of which occur anywhere else in the world. Each exhibits different adaptations and interactions, from the stilt-rooted splendid palm *(Verschaffeltia splendida)* to the massive coco-de-mer *(Lodoicea maldivica)* that is the plant symbol of the Seychelles. With the largest seeds and leaves of any plant, it is surprising how incompletely the biology of this charismatic plant species is known.

Given the complexity of interactions in the web of life, it is best to assume that, in an ideal world, we would not let any species become extinct as a result of our direct or indirect actions. In the world as it is today, at least a third of all plant species are threatened with extinction by the end of the century. Since plants are at the base of the food chain, this places a significant proportion of the animals that depend upon them at risk.

## Where to concentrate our efforts?

Traditionally, reserves and natural parks have been established to protect species and habitats that are at risk. A significant proportion, about 12%, of the Earth's surface has been gazetted as protected areas where endangered species should be able to flourish. It is generally considered best to protect threatened plants or animals *in situ,* that is, where they occur naturally in the wild. For a long time, *ex situ* conservation – in botanic gardens, zoos or other conservation collections away from the natural habitat – has been considered much less satisfactory. This is understandable; in an ideal world we would protect the diversity of life where it naturally occurs. But protected areas cannot be buffered from changes in the global climate, and some of our best efforts to create living space for species in the wild are likely to be undone. This has caused conservationists to

**Below**: Dragon's blood trees *(Dracaena cinnabari)* are among many wonderful endemic plants and animals on Soqotra. The island, which split away from the ancient continent of Gondwanaland around 20 million years ago, has been called 'the Galapagos of the Indian Ocean'. Image: Stephen Blackmore.

# The web of life in the Seychelles

*With colleagues in the Seychelles, I have been collecting information on the range of animals attracted to the coco-de-mer's (Lodoicea maldivica) continuously-flowering male flower spikes that provide an important food resource in the forests. Two different species of lizard feed on the pollen, one of them is a gecko (Phelsuma sundbergii) that jealously guards a male inflorescence during the day. If the lizard is distracted, the Seychelles white slug (Vaginula seychellensis) rapidly comes out of hiding to graze on the male flowers and all the time a range of insect visitors, from honey bees to stingless bees and fruit flies, swarm around taking care to avoid the geckoes that supplement their diet with unwary insects. The dense crown of the palm is crowded with epiphytic ferns and provides living space for a wide variety of other animals. The coco-de-mer is not just one of the most remarkable trees on Earth, it is a microcosm, an ecosystem in itself.*

**Below**: With their famous rhododendron forests, the Hengduan Mountains of Yunnan Province are the richest temperate biodiversity hotspot in the northern hemisphere. Image: Stephen Blackmore.

**Opposite**: An RBGE botanist studies the bryophytes on boulders by Lochain Uaine, Mar Lodge Estate, as part of a bryophyte survey of the estate for the National Trust for Scotland. Image: RBGE/David Long. **Inset**: The northern haircap moss, *Polytrichum sexangulare*, one of the specialised group of tundra mosses restricted to areas of late snow. Image: RBGE/David Long.

rethink their priorities, and has raised the status of *ex situ* conservation. The risk is that, if we ignore the challenges posed by climate change, our primary efforts to conserve nature through protected areas might fail. Increasingly, *ex situ* collections are regarded as vital back-up.

Another fundamental of nature conservation has been the focus on protecting biodiversity hotspots, the places with exceptionally high species diversity. At one level it makes perfect sense to concentrate on tropical hotspots like the Amazon rainforest or the temperate hotspot of Yunnan Province, China – they contain a huge proportion of the total biological richness of the planet. Safeguarding areas in these hotspots can conserve large numbers of species compared, say, to an equivalent area of tundra or boreal forests in northern Europe. Analytical methods have been developed by a number of research groups to identify hotspots

that protect the highest number of species or the greatest evolutionary diversity. Of course the richest places for biodiversity deserve a special degree of protection – it would make no sense to fail to recognise their importance – but equally it would be a mistake to focus exclusively on hotspots. Doing so might lead to the view that there is nothing to save in the far north. Indeed, a report on Europe by one of the largest conservation organisations argued that the Mediterranean region was so rich in plant species, it wouldn't matter if northern Europe was covered with concrete provided the Mediterranean was protected.

Such thinking is nonsense for several reasons. Firstly, it is not strictly true that plant diversity is much lower further north, although there are marked differences in the kinds of diversity in the north and south of Europe (Scotland is one of the richest countries in the world for

# Inside the Conference of the Parties

*In common with other UN Conventions, the progress of the Convention on Biological Diversity is managed through the Conference of the Parties (COP) with the support of a Subsidiary Body on Scientific, Technical and Technological Advice (SBSTTA). The meetings are amazing affairs, with delegates of signatory nations seated in alphabetic order within a giant hall. Further back in the room are organisations and NGOs and, at the very back, the handful of nations who wish to attend but have not adopted this UN Convention. I remember that at COP3 in Buenos Aires in 1996, the appointed Chairman was assisted by spotters using binoculars to see which parties had raised their hands to enter the discussion. Technology now provides delegations with a button to press and a computer places them in an orderly queue. Time is the main constraint and only those parties quickest to request the floor are likely to be called upon.*

Conference of the Parties 9, Bonn, 2008. Image: courtesy of
Botanic Gardens Conservation International.

**Above:** Taking action for a living planet: authors of the Gran Canaria Declaration in 2000.
Image: courtesy of 'Viera y Clavijo' Botanic Garden.

bryophytes – mosses and liverworts). Secondly, whatever the vegetation, ecosystem function is worth preserving everywhere. It is not simply the number of species but their complex interactions that contribute to the overall health of the Earth. In this respect, the planet is like the human body: full function requires all the organs, not just the most complex ones.

For the global garden, our vision needs to concern local outcomes, understanding that one place will be quite different from another in its range of biodiversity and requirements for conservation. Despite superficial similarities of distinctive ecosystems like forests, grasslands, alpine meadows or bogs – features that allow us to recognise such places in the first instance – the mixtures or assemblages of species they contain differ significantly from one place to another. Long-term human efforts should strive to bring about the best possible outcome everywhere, whilst recognising that some densely populated areas will offer much less scope for including nature than those with fewer people and more vegetation. We must aim above all to maintain maximum natural diversity and not to lose any more of the interlocking pieces of nature's jigsaw puzzle. By focusing our efforts on preserving the complex web of life we can preserve the ability of the Earth to recycle and renovate through ecosystem services.

So, how to "tinker intelligently", to use Aldo Leopold's words? How can we achieve a more sustainable relationship with nature? Quietly but persistently and with a growing sense of urgency, the scientific community has begun

to create a strategy for the survival of Earth's biodiversity.

## The remarkable Gran Canaria Declaration

Within a decade of the signing of the Convention on Biological Diversity (CBD), calls for action in response to the biodiversity crisis were becoming increasingly strident. In 1999, at the International Botanical Congress, a six-yearly gathering of the botanical community, Peter Raven, Director of the Missouri Botanical Garden, hosts of the Congress, called for a global response. There was growing realisation that botanists would have to take matters into their own hands and drive the political agenda. Waiting for an international plan to combat plant extinction was not an option. Postponing a coordinated response would simply let the problem get worse.

In response, David Bramwell, Director of the 'Viera y Clavijo' Botanic Garden in Gran Canaria, convened a meeting in April 2000. I was one of 16 people from botanic gardens, the World Conservation Union (IUCN), Botanic Gardens Conservation International (BGCI) and the International Plant Genetic Resources Institute (IPGRI) who met to try to fashion a meaningful way forward. This was an international group with representatives from 14 countries including Colombia, Cuba, Malawi, Mexico, New Zealand, India, the United Kingdom, United States and the Russian Federation, most of whom had worked together before in one international forum or another.

Over the next couple of days, we agreed that we must produce a credible strategy to halt the loss of plant biodiversity. To do that we had to set out key elements to be addressed over a ten-year period. We knew that, to be taken seriously, our short document entitled *The Gran Canaria Declaration* would need to be adopted under the CBD. We were working outside the established framework of national meetings that channelled into the forthcoming Conference of the Parties (COP). As luck had it, our group included Stella Simuyu, then working in the Plant Conservation Programme of the National Museums of Kenya, the host nation for the fifth COP which was to be held in Nairobi the following month. The COP always defers to interventions from developing countries – after all, the CBD is intended to lead to a more equitable sharing of benefits with the developing world. So it was that within a month the representatives of the nations of the world, meeting in Nairobi, found themselves looking at a document drawn up by a group of enthusiasts with no formal mandate. Perhaps to get on with items that were actually on the agenda, they decided (COP Decision V/10) to refer the document to the next meeting of the Subsidiary Body for advice on the merits of the proposal. This propelled our declaration forward faster than even the collection of optimists who had written it could have hoped. By another stroke of fortune, Jameson Seyani, Head of the National Herbarium and Botanic Gardens of Malawi, had just completed a term of office as chair of the Subsidiary Body and was adept at building a consensus ahead of meetings and then networking frantically from the moment delegates gathered until the dust had settled on the final decisions. As a result, decision number Vll/8 of the Subsidiary Body meeting was to recommend the Global Strategy for Plant Conservation, which grew out of *The Gran Canaria Declaration*, for adoption at the next Conference of the Parties in Den Haag in April 2002.

Looking back it still seems astonishing, given the usual ponderous pace of UN Conventions, that within just two years of our gathering in Gran Canaria, the world had agreed on what should be done to prevent its plant resources disappearing into extinction. The stage was set.

If only achieving its 16 targets could be as quick and easy as writing the GSPC had been. But now, at least, each country had guidance to set in place a national response on how to keep their plant diversity. When, later in 2002, notification filtered through from government that there was a new strategy relevant to the Royal Botanic Garden Edinburgh, I felt a certain satisfaction. Botanic gardens and other players around the world have since worked the targets into their own corporate plans and an important shift of emphasis towards plant conservation has taken place. Although the fundamental goal of halting the loss of plant diversity has not yet been achieved, much that is positive has happened, as the next chapter shows.

In 2010, the International Year of Biodiversity, the 10th Conference of the Parties will be held in Nagoya, Japan. It will provide an evaluation of achievements and discuss the framework for the next milestone targets for 2020.

**Above**: *Aeschynanthus chiritoides*. This epiphyte from China and Vietnam was first introduced to RBGE in 2002. Image: RBGE/ Debbie White.

## The Global Strategy for Plant Conservation (GSPC)

The GSPC sets 16 global targets to be met by 2010. Five headings provide an international framework for plant conservation.

### 1 Understanding and documenting plant diversity

**Target 1**: a widely accessible working list of known plant species as a step towards a complete world flora.

**Target 2**: preliminary assessment of the conservation status of all known plant species at national, regional and international levels.

**Target 3**: protocols for plant conservation and sustainable use based on research and practical experience.

### 2 Conserving plant diversity

**Target 4**: effective conservation of at least 10% of each of the world's ecological regions.

**Target 5**: protection of 50% of the most important areas for plant diversity assured.

**Target 6**: managing at least 30% of production lands in a way that is consistent with conservation of plant diversity.

**Target 7**: 60% of the world's threatened species conserved *in situ*.

**Target 8**: 60% of threatened plant species in accessible *ex situ* collections, preferably in the country of origin, and 10% of them included in recovery and restoration programmes.

**Target 9**: 70% of the genetic diversity of crops and other major socio-economically valuable plant species conserved, along with local and indigenous knowledge of their use.

**Target 10**: management plans for at least 100 major alien species that threaten plants, plant communities and associated habitats and ecosystems.

### 3 Using plant diversity sustainably

**Target 11**: no wild flora endangered by international trade.

**Target 12**: 30% of plant-based products derived from sustainably managed sources.

**Target 13**: halting the decline of plant resources and at the same time protecting local and indigenous knowledge, innovations and practices that support sustainable livelihoods, local food security and health care.

### 4 Promoting education and awareness of plant diversity

**Target 14**: incorporating the importance of plant diversity and its conservation into communication, education and public awareness programmes.

### 5 Building capacity for the conservation of plant diversity

**Target 15**: increasing the number of trained people working in plant conservation, according to national needs, to achieve the targets of this strategy.

**Target 16**: networks for plant conservation established or strengthened at national, regional and international levels.

## Progress report as at April 2009, summarised on the BGCI website: www.bgci.org

### 1 Understanding and documenting plant diversity

**Target 1**: excellent progress – target on track for completion in 2010 or soon after.

**Target 2**: limited progress with the classic 'Red List' approach but streamlined approaches starting to appear.

**Target 3**: numerous examples are now available but greater emphasis on dissemination and sharing of experience is needed.

### 2 Conserving plant diversity

**Target 4**: significant progress, 11% of global land area has some degree of protection although effectiveness varies greatly from place to place.

**Target 5**: significant progress, many countries have identified their 'Important Plant Areas' although levels of protection vary and climate change poses additional threats.

**Target 6**: some progress on development of measures for agricultural, horticultural and forest lands.

**Target 7**: limited progress, as with Target 2, too little is known about the status of plant species and the threats they face.

**Target 8**: major progress, the global strategy has served to energise the work of botanic gardens and seed banks.

**Target 9**: substantial progress especially for major crops, for many of which the target has been met. Less progress on other plants of economic importance.

**Target 10**: target met, but climate change is escalating the threat of invasive species.

### 3 Using plant diversity sustainably

**Target 11**: the Convention on International Trade in Endangered Species (CITES) provides an effective mechanism but more research is needed both on threats and on trade.

**Target 12**: significant progress but clear standards and stronger certification schemes are required.

**Target 13**: some progress but threats to local and indigenous knowledge are heightened by environmental degradation.

### 4 Promoting education and awareness of plant diversity

**Target 14**: mixed progress, some countries have developed strong national programmes in support of the strategy, others have yet to respond.

### 5 Building capacity for the conservation of plant diversity

**Target 15**: considerable progress but the lack of human resources continues to be a major constraint on progress in most countries.

**Target 16**: good progress, the global strategy has served to promote networking and has led to the formation of a Global Partnership for Plant Conservation.

**Above**: Contributing to Target 8 of the GSPC, RBGE staff reintroduce the threatened fern *Woodsia ilvensis*, propagated at RBGE, back into the wild at a remote location in Scotland.
Image: RBGE/Heather McHaffie.

# CHAPTER 6

## A GLOBAL SAVINGS BANK

*"A garden is the very best of Savings Banks for, in
return for deposits of time and strength, otherwise
largely wasted, the worker reaps health for himself
and his children in air, vegetables and in fruit."*

Patrick Geddes

# A GLOBAL SAVINGS BANK

In the few years since its introduction in 2002, the Global Strategy for Plant Conservation (GSPC) has redefined the role of botanic gardens. Outwardly things may look much the same to the casual visitor. Botanic gardens still provide what most people seem to come for: fresh air, moderate exercise and contact with nature. These personal benefits are not trivial and a growing body of research shows that spending time in green surroundings really is good for your health. But whilst the botanic garden may not have changed much in appearance, its underlying work is increasingly targeted towards a two-pronged attack on the challenges facing the planet.

On one hand, botanic gardens are altering the holdings of plants in their living collections. In the process of securing a savings bank of wild-origin plants – a living sample of biodiversity – botanic gardens discover, document and defend the plant resources on which we so utterly depend. These collections are then used in research, education and conservation programmes.

On the other hand, the educational programmes of botanic gardens are generally expanding to exploit their great opportunity to engage with visitors, making them powerful engines for social change. As places where families like to spend time, these gardens can

**Facing page:** A Naxi woman washes vegetables at the well in the ancient village of Wen Hai. In accordance with tradition the first and highest pool is used only for drinking water, the second for preparation of food and the third for washing clothes. Image: Stephen Blackmore.

**Below:** An oasis in the city: the innocent pleasures of the botanic garden offer real benefits to the health of young and old. RBGE/ Debbie White.

**Below:** Scotland's international rugby team trains in RBGE's glasshouses – the hottest environment the country could offer prior to the World Cup championships in Australia in 2003. Image: RBGE/Debbie White.

become a rare forum for face-to-face dialogue; real human engagement in an age when so many of our interactions are mediated through liquid crystal displays.

Nowadays, botanic gardens never work alone. They now belong to national, regional and international networks, all of which have adopted the GSPC. Botanic Gardens Conservation International, the largest international network with over 2,000 affiliated gardens, is a powerful coordinating force which estimates that botanic

gardens attract a global audience of more than 200 million visitors each year. Not all of these gardens have an extensive research programme, but for those that do, emphasis is on documenting and understanding the diversity of plant life on Earth. This is important research: exploration of the diversity of life on our green planet is far from complete. Producing an inventory of life on Earth goes far beyond handing out names to each different kind of plant we find. Assigning names is important but it is just a

**Left**: RBGE staff attending the Botanic Gardens Conservation International Congress on Education in Botanic Gardens in Oxford in 2006.
Image: RBGE/Leigh Morris.

## What is a garden?

Samuel Johnson defined a garden as, "A piece of ground, enclosed, and cultivated with extraordinary care, planted with herbs or fruit or food, or laid out for pleasure". This short definition neatly reveals the mindset of the gardener at work; purposefully shaping a piece of the landscape to a preconceived design. Gardens take many forms; the classical gardens of Suzhou, China, were artistic representations of the world in miniature involving interplay between buildings, water, plants and stone. Little Sparta, Ian Hamilton Finlay's garden in the Scottish Borders shown here, is the setting for an extraordinary collection of works of art. Physic gardens grow medicinal plants for teaching and for prescription. Botanic gardens hold scientific collections of plants that are samples of natural plant biodiversity gathered for reference, research, conservation and education. Regardless of purpose or the culture within which they were created, all gardens strive towards a relationship with nature and even when their purpose is essentially utilitarian, they usually have aesthetic aspirations.

**Right**: A garden can be a work of art as well as a labour of love: Little Sparta in the Scottish Borders. Image: Stephen Blackmore.

way of enabling us to share understanding and information. Naming things is something people had to become adept at in order to survive (the world is full of species we find good to eat and others that find us good to eat: it is important to be able tell the difference). Botanic garden science goes beyond mere naming to reconstructing the tree of life: the pattern of evolution through which the complexity of the web of life was assembled.

Each botanic garden makes a different contribution. Let's look now at how the work of the Royal Botanic Garden Edinburgh has developed over the centuries, constantly adapting to the realities of a changing world.

### The Royal Botanic Garden Edinburgh – a local garden on the world stage

The Royal Botanic Garden Edinburgh (RBGE) is unique in Scotland, being both an internationally renowned scientific institution and a popular visitor attraction. Its international standing was reaffirmed in 1999 when botanists of the world gathered at Missouri Botanical Garden in St Louis for their six-yearly Botanical Congress. A poll asked participants which they regarded as the world's most important and influential botanic gardens. The Royal Botanic Garden Edinburgh found itself in distinguished company in the elite group of four top gardens together with the Royal Botanic Gardens, Kew, New York Botanical Garden and Missouri Botanical Garden.

What these four have in common is the size and scope of their collections and the scale and impact of their contribution to research, conservation and education. That the United Kingdom should hold two of the world's leading botanic gardens reflects a long tradition of studying the diversity of life and a national passion for gardening. That Scotland should have the older of these two great gardens and one of the world's richest collections of living

## A potted history of RBGE

**1670**  Physic garden for the cultivation of medicinal plants founded at St Anne's Yards adjacent to Holyrood Palace by Dr Robert Sibbald and Dr Andrew Balfour.

**1676**  More land leased, attached to Trinity Hospital, today site of the east end of Waverley Station. Trinity Hospital Garden placed under care of James Sutherland, appointed first Regius Keeper by William III in 1699.

**1763**  Gardens move to Leith Walk under John Hope (Regius Keeper, 1761-86).

**1820**  Move to part of present site at Inverleith begins under Robert Graham (Regius Keeper, 1820-45).

**1858**  Temperate Palm House built at Inverleith.

**1864**  Garden extended by 4 hectares through acquisition of Experimental Garden from the Royal Caledonian Horticultural Society.

**1876**  Garden extended by 12 hectares through acquisition of land surrounding Inverleith House.

**1889**  Under Isaac Bayley Balfour (Regius Keeper, 1888-1922) the Garden comes under control of the Crown – Her Majesty's Office of Works.

**1892**  Horticulture and forestry courses initiated, lasting two to three years; free tuition in return for labour. These later became the Diploma Horticulture Edinburgh (DHE).

**1929**  Benmore Botanic Garden becomes first Regional Garden of RBGE.

**1969**  Logan Botanic Garden becomes second Regional Garden of RBGE.

**1978**  Dawyck Botanic Garden becomes third Regional Garden of RBGE.

**1999**  Professor Stephen Blackmore appointed as 15th Regius Keeper by Her Majesty Queen Elizabeth II.

**2009**  The John Hope Gateway opens.

plants reflects historical origins during the Scottish Enlightenment. Despite the less than generous reputation of our climate, the reality is that oceanic Scotland provides good growing conditions with ample rainfall and moderate winters, permitting an exceptionally wide variety of plants to be grown outdoors.

## A global network

Today the canvas on which RBGE works is global. In 2009 the living collections include plants from 161 different countries. In the four Scottish gardens of RBGE are growing no fewer than 16,000 species, a remarkable 7% of the world's flora. This represents an extraordinary sample of the world's botanical living inheritance. Almost as diverse in their origins are the three million preserved specimens in the herbarium, which include material from at least 157 countries. Many of these countries have no equivalent collections of their own.

How exactly do botanic garden collections come into being and why are they so valuable? There is a deceptive simplicity to botanic gardens that belies their true importance and the value of the services they provide to society. Collecting wild plants in the field is just the start of a long chain of events that sees a flow of plant material coming into the Garden and then being used for a multitude of purposes. Plants in a botanic garden are not just there to look good, although they can and should be displayed beautifully. Far beyond their aesthetic contribution to the landscape of the garden, the plants are specimens, components of a living collection equivalent to that of a museum, library or art gallery. In common with those collections they can be used for reference, for research and as teaching materials, but unlike them they include living as well as preserved examples (it would be great to be able to grow a few more Picassos or Titians but gallery curators know better than to try taking cuttings from their originals). Having living plant material opens up many possibilities for research and conservation, provides a stream of material for use in educational programmes and presents a self-renewing seasonal attraction that is never quite the same.

**Above:** In remote Himalayan regions, international teams, including RBGE staff, collect seed for living collections and prepare multiple sets of herbarium specimens, carefully dried in plant presses over heat and annotated meticulously. Images: RBGE/David Knott/Mark Watson/RBGE archives.

# The plant specimen value chain

## STEP 6

**Value added:** after passing through many hands and gaining value at every step, the specimen is finally available for use. Through further study it, and the data associated with it, continues to increase in value.

## STEP 5

**Recording:** with the identity of the specimen determined, data is entered into the plant records database. A scanned image is taken. Further expertise is required to place herbarium specimens into the correct sequence, based on the latest DNA-based classification, or to grow the living material.

## STEP 4

**Identification:** it takes years of experience to be able to sort a pile of new specimens according to family and genus. People who can do this with new plants from anywhere in the world have rare expertise. Curatorial staff or specialists provide a final identification. If the specimen cannot be matched in the collection or published literature, it may be a new species, in which case a specialist prepares a technical description for publication based on the new 'type' or definitive specimen.

## STEP 3

**Back in Edinburgh:** further expertise incorporates specimens into the collections. Herbarium specimens are removed from newspapers and mounted on archive-quality card. Arranging and mounting them to display their principal features is a highly developed skill. Seed goes to the nursery for germination and DNA samples to the molecular laboratory for immediate study or long-term storage.

## STEP 2

**Preparing specimens in the field:** herbarium specimens are pressed, dried over heaters and packed in newspapers. Seeds are removed from fruits, cleaned and dried. Specimens are then packed for transportation back to the institute – often with great difficulty from remote locations.

## STEP 1

**Collecting specimens takes a trained eye:** professional collectors carefully select particular plants in the field leaving others behind. They add value by documenting details, noting key features of each specimen and its surrounding plant community. Global Positioning System (GPS) coordinates record the exact locality.

**VALUE**

**TIME AND EFFORT**

**Above**: Time traveller: discovered alive in 1994, the Wollemi pine
*(Wollemia nobilis)* was previously only known from fossils up to
90 million years old. Plants sent by air from Australia were closely
inspected by RBGE staff and quarantined before going on display at
RBGE. Images: RBGE/Lynsey Wilson.

# Giant leaps of faith

When Piers Patrick planted the avenue of giant redwoods (Sequoiadendron giganteum) at Benmore Botanic Garden in 1863 he knew he would not live to see them reach full maturity. He may not have known that, if conditions on Scotland's west coast continue to resemble those on the western seaboard of North America, the trees he was planting might live for over 3,000 years.

Benmore's giant redwoods symbolise a faith in the future that is worth celebrating. It is an example of the gardener's capacity for long-term planning and it is by no means unique. Recently I had the pleasure of visiting Cibodas Botanical Garden on the Indonesian island of Java and seeing an equally bold statement. An avenue of bunya pines (Araucaria bidwillii), planted here in the same decade as the Benmore avenue, is one of the earliest plantings at Cibodas. These too are big, long-lived trees, capable of reaching 50 metres in their native Queensland.

Walking along an avenue of giant trees, whether in Scotland or Java, is a truly moving and uplifting experience. It gives inspiration when we feel hemmed in by the destructive effects of short-term thinking.

**Above:** Benmore's avenue of giant redwoods. Image: RBGE/Lynsey Wilson.

**Left:** Avenue of bunya pines at Cibodas Botanical Garden, Java. Image: Stephen Blackmore.

**Below**: Illustration of *Greenwayodendron suaveolens* by Rosemary Wise from the field guide *Sangha Trees* which enables non-specialists to identify the hundreds of trees found in the Congo rainforest.

We can compare the value of these specimens to the way goods increase in economic worth as they progress from their point of origin to the marketplace. Take the case of a tree, perhaps a mahogany growing in Central America. The subsistence farmer who fells the tree gains a small sum of money by selling it to someone with a timber lorry. The lorry owner takes it to a town where he can re-sell it at significant profit: the tree has already increased in value as a commodity. The buyer may then saw the tree into logs for the local construction industry and make a further profit. An even greater profit can be realised by processing the raw timber, perhaps into furniture or veneer. The value of the tree is much greater than it was before processing and an even higher price can be obtained by exporting the veneer. In just the same way, a value chain for botanical specimens sees specialist expertise being applied at every step from the field to the living or preserved collection. As the specimen progresses from its place of origin deeper into the heart of the collections, it becomes ever more precious; its value growing through continuing research (see the plant specimen value chain on page 90).

## Putting the collections to work

The fundamental mission of botanic gardens is to continue the documentation of plant life on Earth, following a scientific tradition dating back long before the great Swedish naturalist, Carl Linnaeus, established the system used for naming species in the early 18th century. This task – providing baseline information about names and characteristics of species – is an essential foundation for all other sciences. We can't make use of the biological riches of the planet unless they can be recognised and identified with consistency and precision. Equally, we can't begin to assess the status of wild populations of plants or take steps to conserve them under the Global Strategy for Plant Conservation unless we can tell what they are.

In Europe and North America, this approach is taken for granted. The British Isles are better documented than any comparable part of the planet, with an abundance of richly-illustrated books that will allow anyone with reasonable powers of observation to identify any species they see. From the *Observer's Books* to technical manuals, there is a wealth of published knowledge. But how would we fare if we were to find ourselves in the tropical rainforests of the Congo, surrounded by thousands of unfamiliar trees? There are no shortcuts, no ways of avoiding the need for painstaking documentation. Plant specimens must move along the value chain until there is sufficient knowledge to write a Flora, a published account of all the plant species in an area with keys for their identification. With that baseline taxonomic research completed, the knowledge gained can be distilled into simplified systems for identification. In rainforests of the Congo or Sarawak there are now books by RBGE scientists that will enable you to identify the trees around you by looking closely at a single leaf. When biodiversity can be identified by non-specialists its benefits can be exploited in a thousand practical ways. Biodiversity research is not stamp collecting, the knowledge it yields is power.

Biological inventory work feeds directly in to RBGE's second scientific mission: conserving plant biodiversity in the face of global environmental change and mass extinction. In the early years, naturally enough, the focus was on Scottish plants. Botanists from Edinburgh discovered many new additions to the British flora, including the tiny snow-bed herb *Sibbaldia procumbens*, which Linnaeus named in honour of Robert Sibbald, one of RBGE's founders. Today, conservation efforts are targeted at Scottish and British plants, coniferous trees and selected regions of the world where scientists at the Garden have the necessary collections and expertise.

Direct action to conserve threatened plants starts at home and takes the form of Habitat or Species Action Plans. Botanic gardens have a unique resource, namely their practical know-how and expertise in propagation and cultivation, especially of unusual or little-known species. RBGE publishes a special journal, *Sibbaldia,* to capture and disseminate the horticultural expertise of its staff. There have already been many successes. Compared to animals, plants are much easier to raise in captivity and then release back into the wild. The sticky catchfly (*Lychnis viscaria*) has been restored to its former habitat on Arthur's Seat in Edinburgh and the whorled Solomon's-seal (*Polygonatum verticillatum*) has been reintroduced into Glen Tilt in Perthshire from vegetatively propagated material. Elsewhere, the montane fern species oblong woodsia (*Woodsia ilvensis*) and four different kinds of willow (*Salix lanata, Salix lapponum, Salix myrsinifolia* and *Salix myrs-*

## The three scientific missions of RBGE:

- Providing baseline taxonomic and botanical data as a foundation science

- Conserving plant biodiversity in the face of global environmental change and mass extinction

- Understanding the evolutionary processes that have given rise to the world's botanical diversity.

*inites*) are being reintroduced to remote hilly places in Scotland.

Conifers, an ancient group of trees that are important sources of timber in every continent where they are found, are the focus of particular effort. The International Conifer Conservation Programme (ICCP) takes care to collect seed representing genetic diversity found in wild populations, then uses this to establish population-level plantings at safe sites in botanic gardens and on private land. At Benmore Botanic Garden, on the slopes of Glen Massan in Argyll, the project has established a Chilean Rainforest with over 300 threatened conifers including monkey puzzles (*Araucaria araucana*), *Fitzroya cupressoides, Pilgerodendron uviferum, Prumnopitys andina* and *Saxegothaea conspicua*. The trees, still scarcely three metres high, are densely underplanted with Chilean shrubs including the magnificent Chilean flame tree (*Embothrium* species). It's a fine example of long-term thinking and in the decades and centuries ahead this small corner of Scotland will provide protection to populations of plants from the other side of the planet.

*Ex situ* conservation plantings in Benmore's Chilean Glade are complemented by collaborative action on the ground in Chile. Similarly, a century after George Forrest explored the Hengduan Mountains region of north-western Yunnan, RBGE and its twinned institute, the Kunming Institute of Botany, share a flagship conservation effort at the Lijiang Alpine Botanic Garden and Field Station. The key to such projects is partnership with local people. Of course it is not possible for any single institution to tackle the problems of the whole

world. Even so, RBGE has active partnerships in over 40 countries.

Today a vast array of techniques and sophisticated computer programmes underpin RBGE's third scientific mission: understanding the evolutionary processes that have given rise to the world's botanical diversity. The history of life on Earth is contained within living things and it can be teased out. Electron microscopy reveals hidden structures. DNA sequences provide vast quantities of information on shared evolutionary history, parentage of individual plants and, potentially, a powerful tool for identification using DNA barcodes. Each of us and every other living thing has the story of our descent hidden in our form and our DNA.

Spectacular progress has been made since reading and comparing DNA sequences

became routine. Our knowledge of the evolutionary tree of life has advanced more rapidly in the last two decades than in all of human history. An exciting new chapter is opening up now that precise sections of DNA have been found with the potential to provide a unique fingerprint or barcode for each species. If the miniaturisation of electronic equipment continues at its present rate, portable DNA analysers may soon be available for fieldwork. It might then become possible to stand in the Congo rainforest and slip a piece of leaf into a handheld gadget that extracts a DNA sequence, compares it with on-line databases and reveals the identity of the species in question. But this mind-boggling advance would still depend on the skill of taxonomists to work out what everything is. Without reference back to carefully

**Facing page**: The Chilean Rainforest (foreground) at Benmore Botanic Garden is an *ex situ* conservation collection comprising dozens of species collected from the wild that will one day resemble a forest in Chile. Image: RBGE/Peter Baxter.

**Below**: Botanic gardens have a diplomatic role, welcoming important visitors from around the world. Hu Jintao, now President of China, and Eric Milligan, then Lord Provost of Edinburgh, admiring archival materials from China at RBGE. Image: RBGE/Debbie White.

## Botanical twins

China and the Himalayan region have been a focus of interest for RBGE since the late 19th century, when exciting new botanical discoveries by French missionaries such as Pere Delavey and Abbé Soulie came flooding into the herbarium from western China. They pioneered the exploration of the world's richest temperate biodiversity hotspot and stimulated George Forrest, Ernest Wilson and other notable collectors to follow. At that time China had no botanical institutions of its own but it soon began sending botanists to Europe and America. In the 1930s the eminent Chinese botanist, Professor T.T. Yu, established contact with the Royal Botanic Garden and later visited Edinburgh in the late 1940s to work with Sir William Wright Smith. When China re-opened its doors to the outside world his students re-established contact and joint expeditions soon followed. In 1991 RBGE and the Kunming Institute of Botany were twinned and a succession of high profile delegations have since visited Edinburgh including Hu Jintao, now President of the People's Republic of China, in 2001.

curated specimens in herbaria and museums around the world, the answer emerging from the gadget would be meaningless, unconnected with any other fact. Fieldwork would be like beaming down from the Starship Enterprise to an unknown planet and detecting "Life, Jim, but not as we know it". When 'unknown sequence' flashed on the gadget's touchscreen it would represent that eureka moment: the discovery of a new species. But we would remain lost even if we knew the DNA sequence of every living individual, unless we could link this to the knowledge of nature gained by looking at the world and selecting specimens.

## Hope for the future

Today, botanic gardens are in the vanguard of change. Even those that are not very active in research or plant conservation generally have public and schools education programmes. At the Royal Botanic Garden Edinburgh we have recognised that our dual identity as a scientific research institute and an established and popular visitor attraction affords unique opportunities for public engagement. On a fast-changing planet, RBGE plans to exploit these opportunities as fully as possible and has been investing in the interpretation and infrastructure of its four Gardens as well as in its people.

The John Hope Gateway at the West Gate of the Edinburgh Garden commemorates one of RBGE's most celebrated Regius Keepers, an important figure in the Scottish Enlightenment. John Hope lived from 1725 to 1786 and was Regius Keeper when the Garden was at Leith Walk from 1761 until his death. The purpose of the Gateway which bears his name is to inspire hope. Faced by many uncertainties and seemingly insurmountable challenges, the big question, for most people, is how, as individuals, they can make a difference. By providing scientifically accurate information about the natural environment and how it is changing, we hope to help visitors of all ages find the answer to that question.

*The history of life on Earth is contained within living things and, with the right techniques, it can be teased out.*

# PART 3:
## WHERE DO WE GO FROM HERE?

Working in the Demonstration Garden at the Royal Botanic Garden Edinburgh.
Image: RBGE/Lynsey Wilson.

# CHAPTER 7

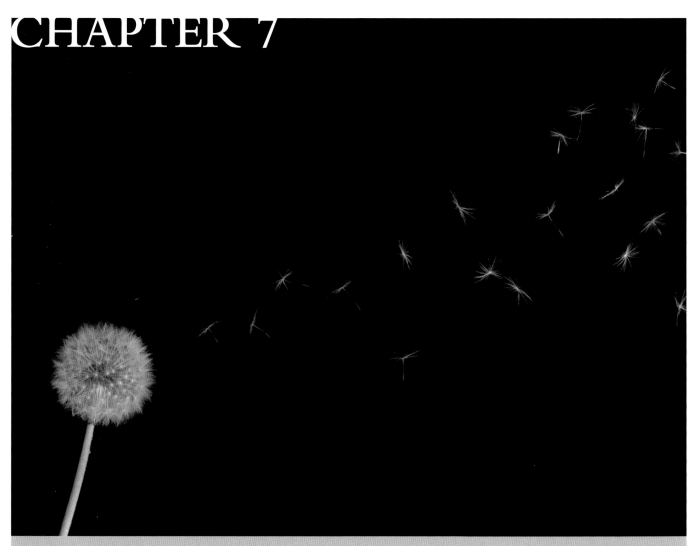

Image: RBGE/Lynsey Wilson.

## WE CAN'T TURN BACK THE CLOCK

Our future will be determined, for better or worse, by our actions or inactions. So let's think like gardeners on a garden planet. Let's act at once but with the long term in mind, working towards a vision that keeps our rich biological inheritance. If we can keep the planet's ecosystems working we can continue to inhabit a green, living world that supports life in an abundance of ways. To succeed we must find a more sustainable relationship with the natural world. We must look forward because we cannot turn back the clock.

# IT'S NOT TOO LATE
# TO ACT!

Today's global environmental challenges are unprecedented in their nature and scale. How then should we meet them? The answer, I propose, is a mixture of optimism and purposeful action. Much of the biological richness of our world, our natural heritage, has already been lost and yet more will follow into oblivion unless we respond urgently.

If we accept that there is no endless wilderness just over the next horizon, how should we adapt to thinking of the world as a garden? Choosing a design for a garden planet is far from simple. It might seem that the best possible outcome would be to restore Earth to its pristine condition, reflecting a particular point in the past. But when exactly would that be?

Assuming we could restore the natural world to any point in the past, where would we aim for? Should we try to re-create conditions that occurred in Europe before the impact of agriculture was felt on the landscape? Or go back even further to the landscape early humans found as they spread out of Africa? Whichever option sounds preferable, neither of them is possible. Extinction has claimed too many pieces of our natural heritage to imagine we could take the Earth back to some previous condition. Even turning the clock back 250 years to the beginning of the Industrial Revolution would prove impossible. In much of Europe forests, wetlands and heathlands have been broken up into too many dispersed fragments for us to rejoin the pieces. To erase human impact on life in the tropics would be even more difficult.

The web of life has been spun over vast periods of time. Efforts to garden the Earth can have no simple objective such as going back to a pre-industrial or pre-human arcadia but must

**Below:** The Jade Dragon Field Station near Lijiang. Image: Stephen Blackmore.

**Below**: In Wuhan Botanical Garden in 2005 with young people – the best and brightest hope for the future. Image: Stephen Blackmore.

**Right**: Looking to the future : though much has been lost, around 2,000 new species of plants continue to be discovered every year. Peter Baxter, Curator of Benmore Botanic Garden, collecting plants in Japan. Image: RBGE/ David Knott.

be bold and intelligent in seeking to achieve a new state of balance in the web of life, allowing biodiversity to regenerate, expand and evolve.

Creating a future in which humans and biodiversity co-exist does not have to mean a hair-shirt existence and giving up the enjoyable things in life. Quite the opposite, there are opportunities for economic prosperity in rising to the challenge. Consumers can make choices that reward and encourage sustainable businesses. Producers can discover new market opportunities providing locally-produced or energy-efficient products. Reducing our energy demands at a personal level is an important step everyone can take. We can be informed citizens, engaged with the real issues of the day and helping to keep political leaders focused on the long-term future, not just headline-grabbing short-term gains. With the power of internet communications everyone is potentially a citizen of a global village. Speaking to

university students in Sichuan just months after the devastating earthquake of 2008, I found them to be well-informed on environmental matters, willing to challenge their leaders and insistent about the need for speedy adoption of alternative energy in China.

Unqualified optimism about the future could be as damaging as denying that the Earth faces problems. Bland reassurances that we can solve the problems of the planet could engender a dangerous complacency. But I am optimistic that we can tackle the challenges *if* we make them our highest priority and *if* we understand that solutions are expensive and require economic levers that drive change in helpful directions. Though people are now stirring for action, humanity is not yet fully committed. Whether we will succeed or fail, time will tell, but whatever the outcome, let it not be for want of action.

# CHAPTER 8

## BUSINESS AS USUAL

The words 'business as usual' reassure and comfort. They tell us that trains will run on time, supermarket shelves will be full and filling stations will have plenty of petrol. In today's globalised world, we have built an elaborate way of life to meet our every need. We devote a great deal of effort to ensuring business as usual.

But this comforting phrase hides a sinister reality. Business as usual now consumes more resources than our planet can produce. To avoid bankrupting nature, we need to redress the balance in favour of the natural economy. We need to restore business as usual from the Earth's perspective, allowing plants to power the natural cycles of production and renewal. This might seem less convenient for us, but it is the only way to meet our needs in the decades ahead. Best of all, we can fashion a future at least as fulfilling and comfortable as today. We might even surprise ourselves and shape a fairer world for all humanity.

I have suggested that the future is up to all of us – collectively if not individually – rather than resting in the hands of an abstract, external 'them'. But it is important to clarify that we cannot have any future we might choose. Our choices are constrained by the history that has brought us to this precise point in time. Even so, there are a huge number of possible futures, depending on how urgently we respond to the unprecedented challenges we face today and with what degree of determination. To keep things simple, I am going to describe just four futures. I am willing to predict there is really only one truly desirable choice.

# WHICH FUTURE WILL
# WE CHOOSE?

Let's imagine there are four gateways standing before us. We have to go through one of them but we need to choose carefully because, once we have gone through some of the gateways, there is no turning back. As discussed earlier, we cannot turn back the clock. As greenhouse gases accumulate in the atmosphere there is no quick way of reducing them, so making the wrong choices now will define our future for centuries.

These gateways are not simply a figment of my imagination. They are based on an image taken from some of the most comprehensive and carefully considered science ever undertaken. The image comes from a chart in *Climate Change 2007: Synthesis Report* published in 2007 by the Intergovernmental Panel on Climate Change (IPCC) – an international committee of specialists established by the United Nations in 1988 and charged with receiving and weighing the latest evidence about climate change and translating it into advice.

This committee draws together the results from a large number of monitoring programmes and experiments around the world. It adopts a cautious and conservative approach to its findings. It would be difficult to imagine a better way to gather intelligence about the condition and prospects of the planet. Yet the IPCC draws criticism from assorted disingenuous websites that pour cold water on its findings and supply reassuring platitudes in the place of factual evidence. Those who scorn the IPCC contend that we have been here before; nature can take care of itself and the climate is only changing as it has always done.

It is human nature to look away from oncoming danger and, after all, wouldn't it be comforting if the sceptics were right? When the IPCC published the *Synthesis Report* in February 2007, they imagined that the strong scientific consensus it contained would provide a wake-up call to society, grabbing our attention and galvanising our actions. Perhaps they had not fully appreciated the human capacity for denial (or how hard it is to engage our at-

tention when we are worried about our home football team facing relegation).

## Four gateways to the future

The *Synthesis Report* itself is quite technical and complicated and, although written for as wide an audience as possible, it may be difficult to understand without the aid of an interpreter. This is scarcely surprising; its scope is a small but rather complicated planet. Don't worry, I am not about to attempt a précis; instead I will focus on a particular chart that captured my imagination. What this chart does is summarise four very different possible futures for humanity and the resulting changes in global temperature. If you would like to dig deeper, the *Climate Change 2007: Synthesis Report* can be found at www.ipcc.ch and for convenience we will follow their colour scheme here.

**Facing page:** Half of humanity now lives in cities but life still depends upon the products of nature. Image: Stephen Blackmore.

**Above:** At the entrance to Shinto shrines, torii gates mark the entrance to sacred space; here they symbolise pathways into the future.
Image:
©iStockphoto.com/Michael Shake.

## Four futures facing our planet

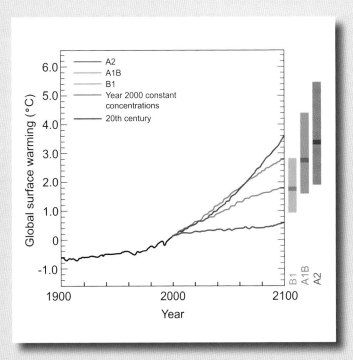

This chart, showing global surface warming between 1900 and 2100, is based on models that reflect interactions between ocean currents and global weather systems.

The black line shows a model of historical warming during the 20th century, the blue, green and red lines show three different future geopolitical scenarios, labelled A2, A1B and B1 (see text for details). The colour-coded bars on the right indicate the best estimate (the solid line within each bar) and the possible range of variation for each scenario. The magenta line is a forward projection based on concentrations of greenhouse gases remaining constant at year 2000 values.

Full diagram and further information at: www.ipcc.ch/pdf/assessment-report/ar4/ syr/ ar4_syr.pdf

**Image:** courtesy of IPCC. Taken from *Climate Change 2007: Synthesis Report.*

The four different coloured lines on the graph model different assumptions about economic and social development in the future and how each course of events would influence global surface warming of the planet. Global warming is, of course, only one component of climate change. Its effects are most likely to be experienced as a greater frequency of extreme weather events and changes to the normal pattern of the seasons. Global warming is simply the headline phenomenon. There will also be very significant differences between the impacts in one part of the world and another.

The IPCC developed 26 future scenarios, grouped into four main families, each presenting variations on a theme of how the geopolitical future of our world might unfold. They incorporate different assumptions for a number of factors including: population levels in developed and developing countries; gross domestic product (GDP); *per capita* income; energy sources; adoption of new technologies, and changes in land use.

They found such scenarios to be the best way to illustrate the diversity of possible futures and used a small selection of the most informative and compelling ones in their *Synthesis Report.* Here we will focus on a single chart that shows four coloured lines representing four alternative futures providing a simple yet powerful way of picturing and exploring the gateways to different futures. It is worth bearing in mind, however, that some scientists say the IPCC is too cautious in its projections and that temperatures and sea levels could rise much further than even the worst case scenarios we will find through these gateways.

### Through the Magenta Gateway to a garden planet

Unlike the other three lines of the chart, the Magenta Gateway is not based on modelling a particular economic and demographic scenario. Instead it represents a projection into

# The Magenta Gateway

To pass through this gateway to a stable world much like the one we live in, we need to:

• Reduce annual carbon dioxide emissions to below seven gigatons (to keep carbon dioxide concentrations below 500 ppm)

• Adjust to a sustainable use of Earth's resources through stabilisation strategies (see next chapter)

Illustration: Sarah Batey.

a future that might have been achieved if we had been able to maintain the balance of atmospheric gases that existed in 2000. We passed the turn of the millennium some years ago now and greenhouse gas emissions have continued to rise, so is it even possible to return to this course? Yes, but it is by far the most difficult gateway to go through, requiring an urgent response and an unprecedented level of human cooperation within and between all nations of the world.

Choosing this pathway into the future would successfully keep the greenhouse effect under control, avoiding a progressive worsening of its future impact. Recent history shows just how difficult this would be to achieve.

In the past few years, human activities have added seven gigatons of carbon dioxide to the atmosphere every year, not to mention other important greenhouse gases such as methane and the chlorofluorocarbons (CFCs) that have also damaged the ozone layer.

It is hard to visualise what seven gigatons of carbon dioxide means in practice. It corresponds to seven billion tons, which is the equivalent of almost ten times the total production of steel in the world today (about 780 million tons per annum). Some of the carbon dioxide is absorbed into various carbon sinks: the oceans and forests of the world. The balance remains as a growing proportion in the atmosphere. However, emissions of greenhouse gases are continuing to rise rapidly year on year. Could we reverse this trend and bring carbon dioxide emissions back below seven gigatons a year? If we assume the present upward trend is inevitable, there might seem to be no possibility of this.

Despite the enormity of the challenges we would face securing this future choice, it is not impossible for us to do. The next chapter introduces a number of strategies for stabilising greenhouse gas emissions, each of which has the potential to save one gigaton of carbon dioxide emissions. We will see that three of these strategies involve protecting and enhancing the natural capacity of plants and nature to lock away carbon.

Gardening planet Earth can save three gigatons of emissions a year. A dozen other strategies each capable of reducing emissions by one gigaton have been identified, suggesting it is possible to achieve the goal of stabilising carbon dioxide emissions at around year 2000 levels. If we succeed in gardening the Earth we can secure the ecosystem services and natural cycles on which life depends. Our reward would be that we keep our living planet, leaving a legacy to our children that we can feel proud of and they can truly enjoy. Beyond a shadow of a doubt, the Magenta Gateway leads to the best future imaginable.

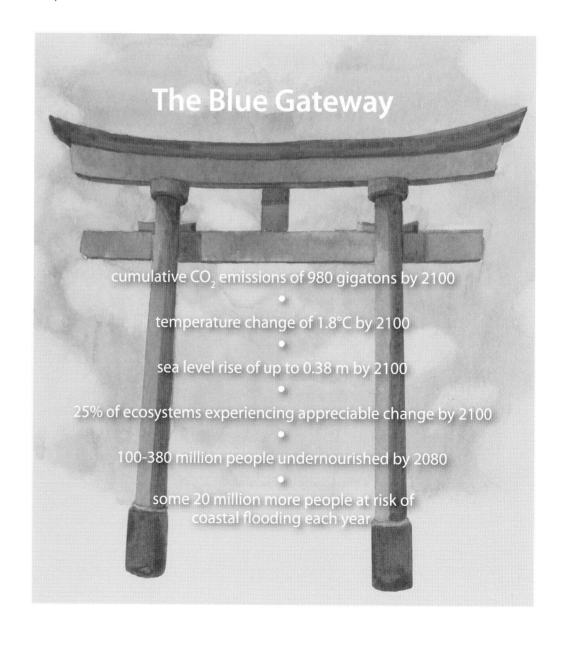

## The Blue Gateway

cumulative $CO_2$ emissions of 980 gigatons by 2100

temperature change of 1.8°C by 2100

sea level rise of up to 0.38 m by 2100

25% of ecosystems experiencing appreciable change by 2100

100-380 million people undernourished by 2080

some 20 million more people at risk of coastal flooding each year

## The Blue Gateway to rising seas and temperatures

The blue line on the chart represents the next best possible future and is based on the IPCC's scenario B1. This assumes that the global human population reaches a peak in the middle of the century and then declines steadily.

Although the human population is continuing to rise relentlessly, there are reasons to believe that this might not, and perhaps cannot, continue indefinitely. Birth rates are falling in developed countries but continue to rise in the developing world where access to birth control may be restricted and children are seen as essential support to families in their old age.

The B1 scenario assumes rapid changes "in economic structures toward a service and information economy, with reductions in material intensity, and the introduction of clean and resource-efficient technologies. The emphasis is on global solutions to economic, social, and environmental sustainability, including improved equity, but without additional climate initiatives". It assumes that our activities continue to add significantly greater quantities of carbon dioxide to the atmosphere each year, but this still represents a lower level of emissions than we are likely to produce if we remain on our business as usual trajectory.

Choosing to go through the Blue Gateway would not be easy but it could be achieved if we place enough emphasis on finding global solutions to economic, social and environmental sustainability and tackling the inequalities between the rich and poor nations of the world. If we really did "make poverty history" rich and poor alike would share the benefits.

The IPCC did not consider which scenario was the most likely to happen, but this might seem a more realistic outcome than the Magenta Gateway. Certainly, the assumed constraint on population growth could be achieved if population trends conform to the most optimistic projections which assume falling family sizes in developing countries, following the trend that developed nations already show. Even so, by the end of this century, the world that lies beyond the Blue Gateway would, on average, be almost 2°C warmer than it was at the beginning of the 20th century.

Would we really notice the difference? That largely depends on where you live. Low-lying coastal areas are likely to be inundated by rising sea levels. The impacts on coastal cities are equally alarming (as we shall see later). So although we would scarcely notice a temperature rise of 2°C in a typical day, if the global average temperature increases by this much the planet will need to do much more than peel off its jumper. Some countries would disappear; none would be untouched.

## The Green Gateway to a shrinking world

This gateway leads into an increasingly different world, with a global surface temperature increase of almost 3°C causing even greater disruption to weather patterns and accelerating the melting of ice caps and glaciers. Here, the IPCC A1B scenario assumes rapid growth in the global economy, with new and efficient technologies quickly coming on stream and human population declining after reaching a peak in the middle of the century. It describes a more equal world in which differences between rich and poor regions are substantially reduced.

The IPCC modelled three different variations of this scenario: one based on the continued intensive use of fossil fuels; another on non-fossil energy sources, and a third, shown by the green line on the chart, on a balance of all sources of energy. Difficult though the world through the Green Gateway would be, it still assumes that we succeed in bringing about significant reductions in greenhouse gas emissions. The prospect of achieving this still looks uncertain. Unpleasant and disturbing though it is, an even less desirable path lies in front of us if we continue with business as usual and fail to respond to the intelligence gathered by the IPCC. It is a future that none of us would willingly enter with our eyes open.

The Green Gateway

cumulative CO$_2$ emissions of up to 1,500 gigatons by 2100

temperature change of 2.8°C by 2100

sea level rise of up to 0.48 m by 2100

30% of ecosystems experiencing "appreciable change" by 2100

100-380 million people undernourished by 2080

some 50 million additional people at risk of coastal flooding each year

### Sleepwalking through the Red Gateway to danger

The Red Gateway leads to an almost unimaginable world. Yet it models the prospects for a future very like the one we are sleepwalking towards at present. We will arrive there if we do nothing to turn away from business as usual.

The Red Gateway leads to a world of political divisions in which the global human population continues to rise relentlessly while different regions develop separately and self-reliantly, intent on preserving their local identities and trying to resolve their own most pressing problems. Economic growth, the introduction of new technologies and increases in *per capita* income are slower than in the other storylines. The world through the Red Gateway would most likely be 3.4°C and perhaps as much as 4.5°C warmer by the end of the century, with temperatures continuing to climb steeply after that.

This would be a world of surprising contrasts, of 'water, water everywhere nor any drop to drink'. A world of deserts and oceans. Not quite the *Water World* of science fiction where dry land is a mythical half memory, but one with no glaciers to feed the great rivers of Asia on which millions depend for water and agriculture.

Sea ice in the Arctic Ocean would be confined to a small area at the North Pole with the ocean largely free of sea ice in summer. Beside the threat of extinction to Arctic animals including seals, walrus and polar bears, the loss of sea ice would spell the end to the traditional way of life of the Inuit people. They, like the peoples of the small island states, are amongst the most vulnerable to climate change, as well as being least able to address the root causes. The melting of the Greenland glaciers would accelerate, with little prospect of being halted.

This fourth gateway is rightly red: for danger. It leads to an impoverished world struggling to support a burgeoning human population. Today's world is far from comfortable for much of humanity, but the world through the Red Gateway is an awful prospect. And a real possibility.

## Business as usual?

So which gateway will we choose? From here, some look easier to navigate than others. The temptation is to keep going in the direction we are currently taking. We like the convenience of business as usual. We have spent a century building up a complex lifestyle that aims to meet our every need. This massive effort supports our busy lives and allows us to concentrate on the things we find important,

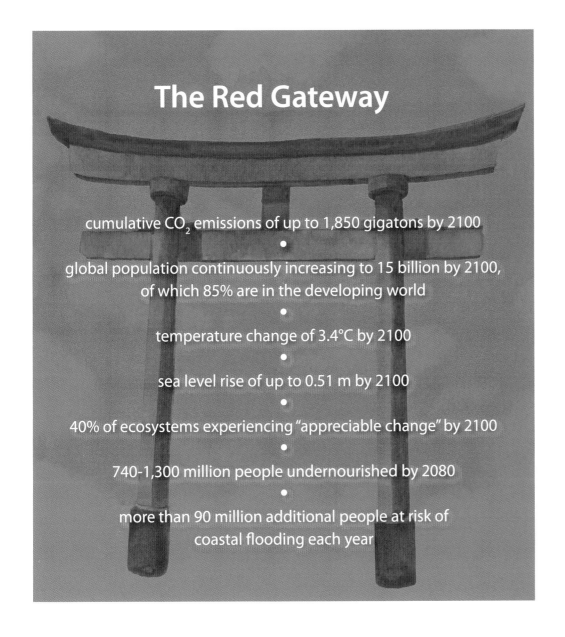

# The Red Gateway

cumulative $CO_2$ emissions of up to 1,850 gigatons by 2100

•

global population continuously increasing to 15 billion by 2100, of which 85% are in the developing world

•

temperature change of 3.4°C by 2100

•

sea level rise of up to 0.51 m by 2100

•

40% of ecosystems experiencing "appreciable change" by 2100

•

740-1,300 million people undernourished by 2080

•

more than 90 million additional people at risk of coastal flooding each year

**Above:** We rely on daily beverages like tea, coffee and cocoa making a long journey to our tables. Tea pickers in Zhejiang Province, China, harvesting the famous Longjing Cha, Dragon Well Tea. Image: Stephen Blackmore.

like shopping, going to the cinema or avoiding relegation to the Second Division. Of course, for much of humanity, business as usual is a hateful grind, a daily struggle to put food into empty bellies. Some 1.2 billion people survive on less than a dollar a day. They don't have the choices we do although they must experience the consequences of our decisions.

A new thought arises: what exactly would business as *unusual* entail? Why do we seem so determined to race blindly towards the Red Gateway? What would it take to follow the route to the Magenta Gateway, giving the planet a future we can look forward to with enthusiasm and optimism?

A thousand different answers clamour for our attention. Alongside the voices denying we have a problem in the first place are others selling quick fixes. One point I hope I have made clear is that there are no simple solutions; the best outcome for the future will involve the combined results of a wide range of actions. We will need all our creativity, determination and resourcefulness to succeed.

If we do manage to keep a world not so different from the one we have today, we will have earned our scientific name: *Homo sapiens.* We won't have to wait long to find out. Even optimistic projections anticipate significant changes to the planet by 2080. Growing life expectancy in the developed world means many of today's children will see the arrival of the future we are choosing and their children will have to live in it. In the early years of the 21st century we still have a choice about when and where we are going. Are we ready to take control?

## We do like to be beside the seaside

Throughout history, living on the coast and at the mouths of major river systems has provided routes for trade and communication: 35 of the 40 largest cities in the developed world are on the coast. More than half of humanity now lives in cities, and an astonishing 40% of us live in coastal cities.

During the 20th century, as global surface temperatures slowly started to increase, the average sea level rose by 17 cm. By the end of the present century, sea levels will rise by at least the same again – and perhaps by as much as an additional half a metre – if we go through the Red Gateway.

It is not simply the additional depth of water that is significant; greater risk comes from tidal surges that put cities as far flung as Alexandria, Cape Town, Dhaka, New York, Lagos, London, Miami, New Orleans, Mumbai, Tokyo and Shanghai at risk. Flash floods caused by extreme weather events and changes in the seasonal patterns of precipitation also hit coastal cities hardest.

Some entire nations, including the Maldives, the Marshall Islands and Tuvalu (formerly the Gilbert and Ellice Islands), comprise low-lying coral atolls that would be erased from the map altogether by a sea level rise of one metre. Their governments are already planning relocation to other lands. It is estimated that a sea level rise of just 90 cm, less than a metre, would make half a million people homeless in low-lying Bangladesh alone.

Global sea level primarily reflects the volume of water locked up in the polar icecaps, the Greenland glaciers and in the 'third pole': the high Himalayas and Tibetan Plateau. The complete melting of the Greenland glaciers could raise global sea levels by a staggering seven metres.

**Right**: The Tweed river in flood beside the entrance to Dawyck Botanic Garden in the Scottish Borders. Will this become a common sight? Image: RBGE/ David Knott.

# CHAPTER 9

## OLD MASTERS IN THE GALLERY OF LIFE

Old growth forests are the crown jewels of nature. If Earth is
a gallery of life these are the Old Masters. They are amongst
the most beautiful places on Earth; the prize of the legacy we
must strive to hand on to future generations. Yet we constantly
undervalue our forests even though we cannot live without
them. Under the Kyoto Protocol the act of preserving old
growth forests is not even taken into account when calculating
carbon emissions. Just making sure they survive is the most
immediate step we can take to counter the greenhouse effect.
This most basic step in gardening the planet is also the most
effective way of maintaining its fundamental ecology.

# THROUGH THE GARDEN GATE

We already have the know-how to avoid the worst outcomes of the environmental challenges that confront us. In practice, we currently lack the commitment, community engagement and political leadership to respond effectively to the global predicament, although there are signs that this is changing. As always, solutions are numerous, complex and interconnected. It is convenient, but not essential, to divide the most effective solutions into two different classes: first, biological remedies concerned directly with gardening the green living world; second, technological solutions based upon human inventiveness and ingenuity.

What's holding us back? It's no surprise that the biggest factor is simply cost. It will be enormously expensive to act. But as the 2006 *Stern Review on the Economics of Climate Change* spelled out: "The benefits of strong, early action on climate change outweigh the costs." Sir Nicholas Stern initially estimated that it would cost about 1% of GDP to stabilise atmospheric carbon dioxide levels at below 500-550 ppm. In 2008 he revised that estimate upwards to 2% of GDP. Even so, if the Earth were valued correctly, we would recognise the bargain this represents. The longer we delay the more the price will rise while scope for action shrinks. If we wait for economically better times before taking decisive action then the price will be paid by our own children, alive now, and not just by great grandchildren we may never know. Given the extraordinary steps that governments can take to support the workings of the global economy, it is obvious that much more can be done to make the investments necessary to maintain the natural economy of the planet. Scottish and UK Government commitments to reducing greenhouse gas emissions by 80% of 1990 levels by 2050 are to be applauded and supported as vigorously as possible. Although this target appears to require a drastic change to our way of life we can achieve this through steady, year on year targets of around 4%.

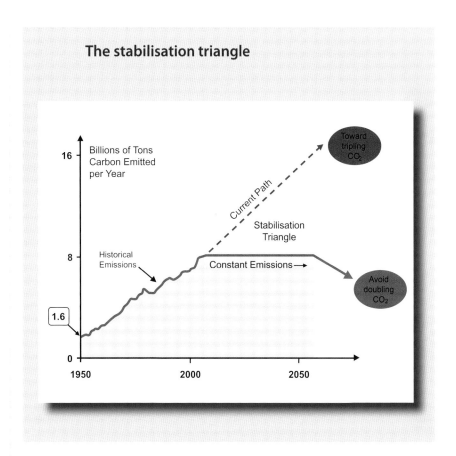

## The stabilisation triangle

### How to build a stable world

Can we reduce emissions to a fifth of 1990 levels? When overwhelmed by complexity, the trick is to break things into manageable sized pieces. One interesting approach is the concept of 'stabilisation wedges'. The idea was introduced in 2004 by ecologist Stephen Pacala and physicist Robert Socolow of Princeton University. Writing in *Science* magazine, they identified a number of strategies already available that could enable us to avoid the worst outcomes of climate change. In their view, consistent with the findings of the IPCC and the *Stern Review*, we need to ensure that carbon dioxide stays below twice the pre-industrial level (which was 280 parts per million).

To achieve that the maximum level of atmospheric carbon dioxide should be kept to within 50 ppm of 500 ppm. In other words we need to keep emissions to the present level or less for the next 50 years and that means cutting projected carbon output by seven billion tons (or seven gigatons) per year by 2055. This might not sound too difficult. But

**Facing page:** *Hazel Coppice*, a painting by Chris Rose. Image: courtesy of Chris Rose.

**Above:** The stabilisation triangle proposed by Stephen Pacala and Robert Socolow. The authors now consider that eight stabilisation strategies will be needed, rather than seven. Image: redrawn with kind permission of Princeton University.

unless developed nations lead the move away from fossil fuels, greenhouse gas emissions are set to continue rising as developing nations, especially India and China, industrialise to adopt higher standards of living for their citizens. Pacala and Socolow divided their 'stabilisation triangle' (see diagram p.117) into seven wedges, each representing a different carbon reducing strategy. Each wedge, they argued, could save a gigaton of carbon dioxide a year by 2055. 'Filling in' all seven wedges over the next 50 years would prevent a doubling of pre-industrial greenhouse gases and this can be achieved in a variety of different ways. In all, 15 different actions were identified. Complete success with seven or mixed success with more delivers the desired result. This approach makes sense because it offers a menu of achievable options. Each strategy can make a substantial contribution to overall success but some will be easier to achieve in full than others.

Three of the wedges involve gardening the Earth. These are biological solutions based on the role of plants in powering the living planet. I will focus more closely on these natural solutions because I see them as the most immediate starting point in tackling both climate change and biodiversity conservation. However, biological solutions alone cannot secure a sustainable future. Technological solutions already available should be added to the mix. By recycling and making efficient use of materials, these solutions fit comfortably with the mindset of the gardener.

## Protect the forests

If we wish to inhabit a green, hospitable planet, powered by photosynthesis, we must protect the forests; it is the simplest and most effective step towards preserving the web of life. Halting destruction of primary forest would save half a gigaton of carbon dioxide emissions a year by 2055, equivalent to a reduction of half a wedge. As things stand, we are on track to destroy half the Earth's remaining primary forest over the next 50 years. Not only should this destruction stop, but botanic gardens, foresters and others should be establishing tree nurseries and extending forests as rapidly as possible.

Not all forests are equal. Tropical forests are about 45% more effective than temperate ones in the amount of energy they capture from the sun and bring into the global ecosystem as sequestered carbon. Tropical forests are also far richer in terms of biodiversity, being home to almost half of all known terrestrial species. By pumping moisture into the atmosphere, they have a profound influence on global weather systems. This does not mean that temperate forests are unimportant. Far from it: the temperate forests of Siberia and Canada are so extensive that they lock up vast quantities of carbon in environments that cannot support the growth of less hardy broad-leafed trees.

Temperate or tropical, the world's most precious forests are old growth forests, preserving the most complex ancient ecological interactions and harbouring significant numbers of species yet to be described. Yet these account for only a third of the planet's standing forest. Since the late 1960s the conventional wisdom in ecology was that old growth forests were

**Below**: Nature has already come up with a device to tackle environmental damage. Image: courtesy of Forestry Commission Scotland and their Convenient Truth campaign.

WIND DEFLECTOR & BUFFERING UNIT

WILDLIFE HABITAT

AIR FRESHENING UNIT

RAINWATER DECELERATOR

CARBON STORE

FOOD PRODUCTION & SELF-REGENERATION SYSTEM

COOLING ZONE

FUEL PRODUCTION UNITS

TIMBER MANUFACTURING PLANT

SOIL STABILISATION SYSTEM

FLOOD MANAGEMENT SYSTEM

SELF-ANCHORING DYNAMIC FOUNDATIONS

carbon neutral having achieved a natural balance between photosynthesis and respiration, between the creation and consumption of energy. It was thought they no longer continued to sequester carbon. Recent studies have shown that old growth forests do indeed go on storing carbon. Old growth temperate forests alone are now estimated to lock away between 0.8 and 1.8 gigatons of carbon every year. This is a hugely important ecosystem service and although the tropical forest contribution has yet to be calculated, it must be even more effective per given area. By gardening the Earth we can go much further. Reforesting 250 million hectares in the tropics and 400 million hectares in temperate regions would save a further full one gigaton wedge of carbon dioxide emissions and go a long way towards restoring the forest cover our planet enjoyed before the explosive growth of human populations.

**Above**: Contributing to Target 7 of the Global Strategy for Plant Conservation: plants propagated in the nursery of the Jade Dragon Field Station to boost wild populations in the surrounding mountains.
Image: RBGE/ David Paterson.

## Action for forests by 2055

- Protecting existing forests could save half a wedge of emissions.

- Restoring Earth's forest cover could save a whole wedge of emissions.

### *Nurture the soil*

An entire wedge of carbon could be saved by managing the world's agricultural soils in ways that build rather than reduce their carbon content. Soil is alive. People often denigrate it as dirt when it should be seen as the global recycling system for nutrients and trace elements. By opening up natural vegetation to cultivate crops we lose up to half the carbon stored in living organisms and decaying organic matter in soil. Plants actively exude organic compounds into the soil through their roots and into a soil ecosystem of great complexity.

It matters that soil carbon stays put. In the context of climate change a worry of as yet uncertain proportions concerns the release of methane, a potent greenhouse gas, from frozen soils in the permafrost of high latitudes and altitudes. One recent study based on pits dug at over a hundred sites in Alaska reported an average of 35 kilograms of carbon per square metre, up to a third more than had been assumed in earlier estimates. Whether greenhouse gases remain trapped in permanently frozen soils will depend on the overall success of our efforts to reduce climate change. Agricultural practices are more amenable to change. Some methods of agriculture rapidly deplete the organic content of soils, others protect against erosion by planting crops to cover the soil and allow carbon content to increase.

## Action for soils by 2055

- Retaining carbon in the soil could save a whole wedge of emissions.

## Plant the right biofuels in the right places

Before we started to exploit fossil fuels all our energy was obtained by burning timber, charcoal or peat. Even today, firewood is the primary fuel for many people although gathering it becomes increasingly challenging. Biomass or biofuels could theoretically contribute a full wedge of carbon savings but that would take about one sixth of the world's available cropland. On a hungry planet this is simply unacceptable which explains the recent backlash against biofuels, once presented as an effective alternative to fossil fuels.

We cannot have our cake and eat it. Plants grown for biofuels cannot also be eaten and in many cases the production of biofuels removes food from the human food chain. The earliest and most extensively used biofuel is bioethanol derived from sugar cane and more recently from maize, which has a lower yield. Brazil was one of the first countries to develop a bioethanol industry based on sugar cane and it expanded rapidly when petrol prices soared in the 1970s. (Henry Ford's famous model T could run on bioethanol or petrol or a mixture of both. Petroleum came to dominate when it could be regarded as a cheap fuel.) Preparing bioethanol from maize, a staple food in Central America now widely grown in Africa and elsewhere, means less maize to feed hungry people. Worse, oil palm plantations for biofuels tend to be planted as replacements for lowland tropical rainforest, squandering biodiversity benefits for short-term profit. However, not all biofuels are bad and they certainly have a part to play in a complex mix of fuels. Where there is a photosynthetic product that cannot be eaten or comes from land unsuitable for conventional farming, they do represent a gain. One example is woodchip from low quality timber such as that from spruce plantations in Scotland. When the fuel is burned, carbon dioxide is released again so, ideally, woodchip should be produced from continuous plantings. In all solutions, a

**Below**: Practicing what we preach: the new Visitor Centre at Dawyck Botanic Garden and the John Hope Gateway in Edinburgh both use woodchip biomass boilers and both use timber in their building construction, locking away carbon in their structures. Images: RBGE/ David Knott.

**Facing page**: Small changes make a big difference: energy efficient lightbulbs are a change that all domestic properties could adopt. Image: RBGE/Lynsey Wilson.

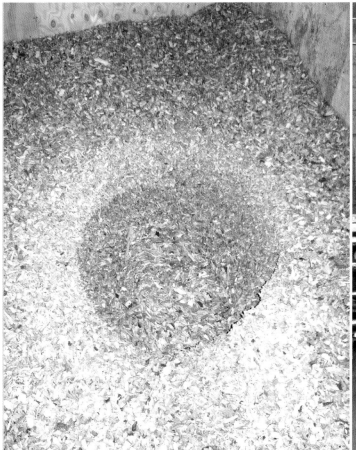

complex mix is required and what suits in one region may not in another.

Biofuels could take a sixth of Earth's cropland to save a wedge but grown in the right place they could help reduce carbon emissions.

## Invest in energy efficiency

Amongst non-biological strategies, energy efficiency is the clear front-runner. Because we have tended to assume that fossil fuels are cheap and almost infinite we have not bothered too much about how quickly they are consumed. Until relatively recently our ignorance of the greenhouse effect excused this oversight. Now perhaps we feel hopeless, as insignificant as an ant in a vast ant colony. But the collective weight of individual actions can solve these problems, just as the force of human numbers created them. As consumers, our choices drive markets and decide the future.

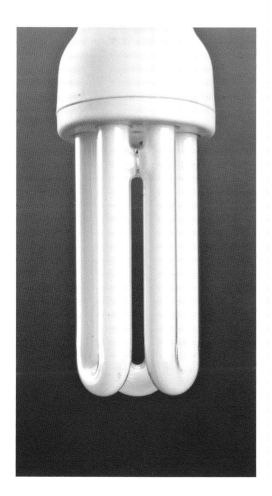

Inside the home there is much each of us can do to reduce our own carbon footprint. Tackling energy inefficiency is also an important economic opportunity, given that much of our existing building stock, vehicles and domestic appliances are very energy inefficient. There is money to be made in energy efficiency. Better building standards produce better homes and workplaces, vehicle emissions legislation encourages more fuel-efficient cars. Securing a 25% increase in the energy efficiency of commercial and residential buildings through better insulation could save an entire wedge. Insulating walls, lofts and windows will make a difference to household bills and contribute to a greater global goal.

Outside the home, switching to energy efficient vehicles could save one entire wedge even with more cars in the world. Another wedge could come from reducing the world's total car journeys by half. In the developed world, car usage is starting to fall in cities with good public transport. On the other hand car sales are booming in the emerging economies. Rising energy prices are driving manufacturers to see new ways of saving energy as a competitive advantage. Hybrid cars have become fashionable and there has been a backlash against 'gas guzzlers'.

### Action for energy by 2055

- Better insulation could save one wedge of emissions.

- Energy efficient vehicles could save one wedge of emissions.

- Reducing the world's car journeys by half could save one wedge of emissions.

Other gains are being made. Rail transport looks to a future of engines that generate steam by burning diesel or gas-oil and trains that store kinetic energy while braking to use when accelerating. People can adapt too. Every time we walk or cycle rather than take the car we make a difference. Car-sharing and using

Image: courtesy of Pelamis Wave Power Limited.

### Pioneered in Scotland

The Pelamis wave power system developed in Scotland, and named after a genus of sea snake, is a promising development that exploits wave rather than tidal power. The three Pelamis machines recently installed in Portugal should be able to generate 2.25 megawatts and, for countries with coastlines, larger installations may be very attractive. Scotland has a huge resource of wave, tidal and wind energy that can be exploited as a major source of alternative energy in the future.

public transport also improve efficiency. But there is a clear role for government leadership as well as individual choice. Only an absurd distortion of the true cost makes it cheaper to fly between cities in Britain than to travel by train. Air travel makes little sense for short journeys over land. Having invented the railways, it is a sad reflection that Britain's rolling stock seems increasingly antique compared to that of many countries.

### Switching away from fossil fuels

There are a growing number of alternative energy sources. Choosing to buy them creates new business opportunities. Switching away from coal-fired power stations and generating electricity in other ways represents a major climate stabilisation strategy. A welcome bonus from not using oil-fired powered stations would be the option to use the planet's finite resources of oil as raw materials for the petrochemical industry. Oil is not just something that burns! Coal is the most polluting of fossil fuels; switching from coal to natural gas at a global scale could save a gigaton of carbon dioxide. A significant component of the current energy mix comes from nuclear reactors. They polarise public opinion like little else but are not direct producers of carbon dioxide emissions. We could do without nuclear power if our conversion to renewable energy is rapid enough but, for now, we should look calmly and carefully at the future before rejecting continued use of nuclear power.

Switching entirely to renewable energy is highly desirable and there are many ways to do it. We can harvest the energy of the sun although it would take 20,000 square kilometres of photovoltaic cells to generate enough electricity to save a single wedge. But photovoltaic cells are dropping steadily in price and have the potential to be incorporated into more and more surfaces.

A dramatic scaling up of wind turbines to 30 times their present level of output, in place of coal-fired electricity, would save a further wedge. Even though wind turbines typically average around one fifth of their potential output, their contribution is not to be sniffed at. So it is not surprising that they are being built at an extraordinary rate with global capacity growing by 25% in each of the last five years. The United States alone added an additional 5.3 gigawatts of capacity in 2007 providing over a third of its new energy output. But this is nothing compared to the 225 gigawatts of wind power progressing through the US planning process. Right now the limiting factor is the actual availability of turbines. Not surprisingly more companies are entering this market. The global resource of wind energy is estimated to be hundreds of terawatts (a terawatt is a million million watts) but this resource is not evenly distributed. Countries like Britain that border the oceans have the greatest potential. Although Britain has yet to match the capacity of some other European countries it has the largest wind resource in Europe. Of course wind turbines are controversial and their siting requires great care and a careful balancing of short and long term interests. However, there can be no doubt they are necessary – perhaps locating them offshore is the best compromise.

And there is much more potential to come with developing technologies. To take just one example, Pacala and Socolow also identified the potential to save three whole wedges by capturing carbon dioxide and locking it away in geological strata that previously held oil, gas or water. To repeat, it will not be easy to give

up our addiction to fossil fuels but every thin slice shaved off each wedge takes us towards a more stable future.

### Action for technology by 2055

- Switching from coal to natural gas could save a wedge of emissions.

- Carbon capture and storage could save three wedges of emissions.

**Above:** Sculptural and symbolic, the Quiet Revolution vertical wind turbine on the John Hope Gateway signals RBGE's commitment to a sustainable future and demonstrates the role of micro-generation on city buildings. Image: RBGE/Hamish Adamson.

# On the trail of pioneers

In 2001, on the first of many visits to the Yulong Xue Shan, or Jade Dragon Snow Mountain, in Yunnan we set off from the village where Joseph Rock lived in the 1920s and 1930s. The house where he gathered his plant specimens and documented the life and language of the local Naxi people is now a museum. Hiking along steep paths through pine forest we came to an open meadow where local shepherd boys perched on isolated boulders to watch their flock – and avoid the leeches. I paused for breath to photograph Sir Anthony Galsworthy, British Ambassador to China, and his wife, Lady Jan Galsworthy, below the jagged spine of the Jade Dragon before we pressed on towards a high meadow.

Later, in the archive collection at RBGE, I saw George Forrest's picture of the same view taken almost a century before. We had been standing near one of his campsites, looking at walking trails he would have known intimately. Remarkably little had changed in the intervening years, although mature fir trees have gone and upper slopes are now often bare of snow.

# GARDENING THE EARTH – CONCLUSIONS

The challenge for the 21st century is to tend the soil and keep Earth green. By gardening the Earth we can secure the best possible future for our own species and for all others. Where do we start? Let's look again at the key elements of the mindset of the gardener.

1. **Long-term thinking.** Gardeners work according to a plan they might not live to see.

2. **Vision.** Gardeners work to achieve their vision, they don't just wait for it to happen.

3. **Connection.** Gardeners have a deep sense of place.

4. **Recycling.** Gardeners are the ultimate recyclers.

5. **Determination.** Gardeners are determined, sometimes to the point of stubbornness.

6. **Responsibility.** Gardeners accept responsibility for their patch.

The natural inclination of gardeners to share what they have and to recycle what they no longer need is the key to the future. People are generally getting better at domestic recycling although we still get far too much unwanted packaging. Paying for less packaging and recycling what remains is the level at which everyone can make a difference. But we need to be more efficient in the first place. An urgent programme is needed to redress the assumption that energy is plentiful and cheap. Spending wisely is essential too. Imagine that each pound, euro, dollar or yuan is a bargaining chip in the future of the planet. Now, stop imagining – it really is. Our choices drive markets and decide the future. Energy choices have particular impact. Right now energy is costing the Earth more than ever. It is astonishing to realise what a difference it makes to live in well-insulated homes. We must use our current but finite plenty as our platform for renewables. We are not plants, we can't photosynthesise but we can learn from plants and harvest the renewable energy resources of the planet. Humankind must end its dependence on fossil fuels. None of this will be easy but gardeners are tough, they can pull weeds until none remain. As gardening guardians of the planet we must stubbornly persist in challenging ourselves to take action for a green living world and demand nothing less from our elected leaders. The future is our collective responsibility.

Each gardener can make a difference to an individual plot of ground but together we can communicate a message that can change the world. How we tend our gardens can become a metaphor for the way we treat the planet. Everyone with a window box, a balcony, a patch of land or a botanic garden can play a part. All the world's a garden and ultimately perhaps there are no better examples of gardening than nurturing the soil and protecting and planting forests.

## Gardening the soil

To sum up, this is where gardeners come into their own. On a small scale we know how to improve the quality of the soil. Just about everything we do in our own domestic gardens, from making compost to adding organic material, can be scaled up and applied to a small planet. By caring for the soil we nurture a rich but unseen portion of life on Earth. Soil life forms are extraordinarily diverse but being out of sight and out of mind they are rarely surveyed. A single gram of soil from Norway was estimated to contain more than four million different bacteria. Almost a third of all the world's known species of protozoa were found in a five-year investigation of soil biodiversity at Sourhope in the Cheviot Hills. Astonishingly, Dawyck Botanic Garden in the Scottish Borders is one of the world's most completely surveyed sites for soil fungi. Our exploration of the planet's soil has only just begun.

## Gardening the forests

We end where we began, with the leaf factory. Every one of us should think twice about a leaf and celebrate it as the "chief product and phenomenon of life". The more heavily wooded the planet, the more the leaf factory can do for the complex web of life on which we all depend. So whether it be densely planting the concrete corridors of motorways and trunk roads or greening our inner cities, let us plant trees wherever possible.

In the urban environment, now home to more than half of all humans, trees provide many benefits beyond their ability to soak up carbon dioxide. They also help to remove pollutants, provide shade and encourage wildlife. Trees in urban streets and gardens are our only antidote to the lava-like flow of concrete that engulfs our cities in the wake of the motor car. Study after study confirms that living with an outlook onto green space is better for human health. Whilst planting trees can be one of the longest-term gestures a person can make, the planter soon reaps more immediate benefits. An apple tree will yield fruit in a few short years – and we have but a few short years to secure our green and healthy world. Let's get planting!

**Right**: Passing on the world of plants to a new generation. A seedling of blue heath (*Phyllodoce caerulea*), a threatened species restricted in Scotland to only a few locations in the Highlands, in RBGE's Nursery. Image: RBGE/ Lynsey Wilson.

## Visionary thinking

Through Millennium Forest for Scotland (1994–2001), new life has been breathed into the ancient Caledonian forests with the dream that, "In a thousand years they will say that there's a forest from Skye to Galloway, from Cape Wrath to the banks of the Tay". We might be pleasantly surprised by how quickly the benefits accrue. In many places the simple expedient of excluding deer has led to rapid regeneration from the soil seed bank. This has worked like a miracle even in places where not a single sapling stood under ageing Scots pines. Best of all, the emphasis is on native trees, providing food for native insects and birds and interacting with soil fungi.

Image: courtesy of Millenium Forest for Scotland.

## Sowing seeds of diversity

Botanic gardens have a special part to play in tree-planting. They are centres of expertise in growing the full diversity of vegetation not just the usual candidates for traditional plantations. They also care where the seeds come from. Their seed banks focus on sampling the genetic diversity within wild populations that provide the key to future adaptability. The International Conifer Conservation Project (ICCP) is just one example of a growing global collaboration of botanical and horticultural know-how. The Royal Botanic Garden Edinburgh works to share its expertise with partners in over 40 countries, including Bhutan, Chile, China, Laos, Nepal, New Caledonia, Oman (above), Peru and the Republic of Yemen.

Image: RBGE/Leigh Morris.

**Beneath the surface, a largely unexplored realm**

At Dawyck Botanic Garden, so far over 1,055 different species of fungi have been found in Heron Wood (above), one of the most thoroughly surveyed sites on Earth. There is still much more to be discovered.

Image: RBGE/ Lynsey Wilson.

Barack Obama 'to reverse Bush policies on climate change'

### A sense of responsibility

One of the brightest signs of hope is the serious commitment political leaders are now showing to reducing greenhouse gas emissions. The message of the *Stern Review* – acting now will cost less than paying the price later – has been received. Scottish and UK governments have both proposed 80% reductions in greenhouse gases by 2050. US president Barack Obama made the same commitment in his 2008 election campaign. Impossible? Not if tackled in bite-sized pieces. We can do it by making year on year reductions of 4%, but we need to start now.

129

# EPILOGUE

Have the fields and brooks of my childhood vanished forever? Do we now inhabit a world poorer than the one we were born into? The answer is both yes and no.

Much has gone. The dominance of the human race has put nature on the retreat and accelerated the extinction of many other species. Forests, grasslands and wide open spaces have contracted while agricultural landscapes and cityscapes have expanded, sometimes from horizon to horizon. Half of us are city dwellers now, and for many the countryside, whether it be farmland, moorland or woodland, is simply a place to visit at the weekend or on holiday. If we see the green of nature from one week to the next it is likely to be the house plant that makes our living room worthy of that name, our own back garden or perhaps the local park. We may be lucky enough to live near a botanic garden that reminds us of the glorious diversity of nature.

Much also remains. Some species have learned to share our urban and agricultural landscapes. Nature can sometimes be surprisingly adaptable, and we are discovering that cities can be green places too. If space is set aside for trees, parks and gardens, both the quality of life and health of people who live in cities are improved. The countryside is still there and now we are learning that agricultural landscapes can produce environmental benefits as well as food. Beyond, there are wilder places. Quieter perhaps than when a full chorus of wildlife lived there. But now we are bringing some former residents home, reintroducing some species to their native environments; reversing past misfortunes. And if we travel far enough the Earth still has its rainforests, savannas, alpine meadows and mangrove forests, its coral reefs and unspoiled coastlines.

This is a world that never stands still. Extinction is part of the natural order, just as diversification is. Humankind was not responsible for the extinction of dinosaurs and except in our imaginations no human ever saw one – though we have all seen their living relatives and delight in encouraging them into our gardens with bags of peanuts and scraps from our tables. We are now, however, responsible for changing the balance of nature much more rapidly than happened before the arrival of our species, except when rare natural catastrophes occurred. All previous extinction crises in the Earth's long pre-history seem related to cataclysmic events like collisions with meteors. Our gradual influences over the millennia and our relatively recent explosive increase in numbers have placed up to 40% of all living mammals and at least 30% of all plants at risk of extinction. It is hard to imagine human life in a world robbed of such high proportions of its other residents. Invisible changes are happening too. We cannot sense the increased carbon dioxide in the atmosphere any more than we could sense the ozone hole expanding. But we can see and measure its effects on nature.

It is clear that the preservation of life on Earth is up to all of us alive today. It is no longer even true to say that we must act for the benefit of future generations. The time for action is now and our success or failure will be seen and felt by people already born.

The backfields behind my first childhood home are smaller now, new streets with new houses lie beyond the brook. But the brook itself still winds through green fields and the wet patch of rushes I knew to avoid remains. Even the enormous oak in the field behind our house still stands, slowly storing carbon in its timber, providing shelter and food to a host of species. It has taken the last half century easily in its stride. I hope the next half century will be so kind.

**Right**: The fields where I ran wild as a child remain today. Image: Google Earth. **Inset**: The oak tree near my house in the winter of 1962-63. Image: Stephen Blackmore.

# FURTHER READING

The data throughout this book were extracted from various sources available to the author up to April 2009. More information can be found in the sources below.

## Publications

Adams, D. & Cawardine, M. 1990. *Last Chance to See…* William Heinemann Ltd., Portsmouth, NH.

Balouet, J.-C. & Alibert, E. 1990. *Extinct Species of the World: Lessons for our Future.* Charles Letts & Co., London, UK.

Blewitt, J. 2008. *Understanding Sustainable Development.* Earthscan Publications Ltd., London, UK.

Carson, R. L. 1962. *Silent Spring.* Houghton Mifflin, Boston, MA.

Colwell, R. K., Brehm, G., Cardelús, C. L., Gilman, A. C. & Longino, J. T. 2008. Global warming, elevational range shifts, and lowland biotic attrition in the tropics. *Science* **322**: 258-261.

Costanza, R., d'Arge, R., de Groot, R., Farber, S., Grasso, M., Hannon, B., Limburg, K., Naeem, S., O'Neill, R. V., Paruelo, J., Raskin, R. G., Sutton, P. & van den Belt, M. 1997. The value of the world's ecosystem services and natural capital. *Nature* **387**: 253-260.

Dessler, A. E. & Parson, E. A. 2006. *The Science and Politics of Global Climate Change: a Guide to the Debate.* Cambridge University Press, Cambridge, UK.

Diamond, J. M. 1998. *Guns, Germs and Steel: a Short History of Everybody for the Last 13,000 Years* (new edition). Vintage, Colchester, UK.

Diamond, J. M. 2005. *Collapse: How Societies Choose to Fail or Survive.* Allen Lane, London, UK.

Dow, K. & Downing, T. E. 2007. *The Atlas of Climate Change: Mapping the World's Greatest Challenge* (revised edition). Earthscan Publications Ltd., London, UK.

Erwin, D. H. 2008. *Extinction: How Life on Earth Nearly Ended 250 Million Years Ago.* Princeton University Press, Princeton, NJ.

Fletcher, H. R. & Brown, W. H. 1970. *The Royal Botanic Garden Edinburgh 1670-1970.* HMSO, London, UK.

Garvey, J. 2008. *The Ethics of Climate Change: Right and Wrong in a Warming World.* Continuum International Publishing Group Ltd., London, UK.

Goodall, C. 2007. *How to Live a Low-carbon Life: the Individual's Guide to Stopping Climate Change.* Earthscan Publications Ltd., London, UK.

Goodman, J. 2006. *Joseph F. Rock and His Shangri-La.* Caravan Press, Hong Kong.

Hamilton, A. C. 2004. Medicinal plants, conservation and livelihoods. *Biodiversity and Conservation* **13**: 1477-1517.

Harris, D. J. & Wortley, A. H. 2008. *Sangha Trees: an Illustrated Identification Manual.* Royal Botanic Garden Edinburgh, Edinburgh, UK.

Hawkins, B., Sharrock, S. & Havens, K. 2008. *Plants and Climate Change: Which Future?* BGCI, Richmond, UK.

Hope, A. 2004. *John Hope, 1725-1786: Scottish Botanist.* Ann Hope, Edinburgh, UK.

Janzen, D. H. 2001. Latent extinctions – the living dead. In: Levin, S. A. (ed.). *Encyclopedia of Biodiversity* (volume 3). Academic Press, New York, pp. 689-699.

Johnson, S. 1805. *A Dictionary of the English Language: in which the Words are Deduced from Their Originals, and Illustrated in Their Different Significations, by Examples from the Best Writers, to which are Prefixed a History of the Language, and an English Grammar.* Longman, Hurst, Rees & Orme, London, UK.

King, D. & Walker, G. 2008. *The Hot Topic: How to Tackle Global Warming and Still Keep the Lights on.* Bloomsbury Publishing Plc., London, UK.

Knoll, A. H. 2003. *Life on a Young Planet: The First Three Billion Years of Evolution on Earth.* Princeton University Press, Princeton, NJ.

Leakey, R. E. & Lewin, R. 1996. *The Sixth Extinction: Biodiversity and its Survival.* Weidenfeld & Nicolson, London, UK.

Leopold, A. 1968. *A Sand County Almanac and Sketches Here and There* (enlarged edition). Oxford University Press, New York.

Lovejoy, T. E. & Hannah, L. (eds.). 2005. *Climate Change and Biodiversity.* Yale University Press, New Haven, CT.

Lovelock, J. 1988. *The Ages of Gaia: a Biography of Our Living Earth.* Oxford University Press, Oxford, UK.

Lovelock, J. 2006. *The Revenge of Gaia: Why the Earth is Fighting Back – and How We Can Still Save Humanity.* Allen Lane, London, UK.

Lusby, P. S. 2003. The role of botanic gardens in species recovery: the oblong *Woodsia* as a case study. *Sibbaldia* **1**: 5-10.

Luyssaert, S., Schulze, E. D., Borner, A., Knohl, A., Hessenmoller, D., Law, B. E., Ciais, P. & Grace, J. 2008. Old growth forests as carbon sinks. *Nature* **455**: 213-215.

Lynas, M. 2008. *Six Degrees: Our Future on a Hotter Planet.* Harper Perennial, London, UK.

Margulis, L. 2000. *What is Life? The Eternal Enigma* (new edition). University of California Press, Berkeley, CA.

May, R. M. 1988. How many species are there on earth? *Science* **241**: 1441-1449.

Mayewski, P. A. & White, F. 2002. *The Ice Chronicles: the Quest to Understand Global Climate Change.* University of New Hampshire, Durham, NH.

McLean, B. 1999. *George Forrest: Plant Hunter.* Antique Collectors' Club Ltd., Woodbridge, UK.

Meine, C. & Knight, R. L. (eds.). 1999. *The Essential Aldo Leopold.* University of Wisconsin Press, Madison, WI.

Miller, A. G. & Morris, M. 2004. *Ethnoflora of the Soqotra Archipelago.* Royal Botanic Garden Edinburgh, Edinburgh, UK.

Millennium Forest for Scotland Trust. 2001. *Millennium Forest for Scotland Trust, Return of the Natives.* Millennium Forest for Scotland Trust, Glasgow, UK.

Mittermeier, R. A. 2005. *Hotspots Revisited: Earth's Biologically Richest and Most Endangered Terrestrial Ecoregions.* Chicago University Press, Chicago, IL.

Morton, A. G. 1986. *John Hope 1725-1786: Scottish Botanist.* Edinburgh Botanic Garden (Sibbald) Trust, Edinburgh, UK.

Muir, J. 1992. *The Eight Wilderness-Discovery Books.* Hodder & Stoughton, London, UK.

Newman, M. F., Svengsuksa, B. & Lamxay, V. 2007. *Selected Resources for Plant Identification in Lao PDR.* Royal Botanic Garden Edinburgh, Edinburgh, UK.

Nicholls, A. & Opal, C. 2005. *Fair Trade: Market-driven Ethical Consumption.* Sage Publications Ltd., London, UK.

Oldfield, S. 1994. *Protecting Plants and their Habitats under the EC Habitats Directive.* Plantlife, London, UK.

Pacala, S. & Socolow, R. 2004. Stabilization wedges: solving the climate problem for the next 50 years with current technologies. *Science* **305**: 968-972.

Reed, A. W. 1999. *Aboriginal Myths, Legends and Fables* (new edition). Reed Natural History, Chatswood, Australia.

Ronald, P. C. & Adamchak, R. W. 2008. *Tomorrow's Table: Organic Farming, Genetics, and the Future of Food.* Oxford University Press, Oxford, UK.

Royal Botanic Garden Edinburgh. 1992. *Four Gardens in One.* The Stationery Office Ltd., Edinburgh, UK.

Ruddiman, W. F. 2007. *Earth's Climate: Past, Present and Future* (second revised edition). Palgrave MacMillan, Basingstoke, UK.

Sayer, J. & Campbell, B. 2003. *The Science of Sustainable Development: Local Livelihoods and the Global Environment.* Cambridge University Press, Cambridge, UK.

Scharlemann, J. P. W. & Laurence, W. F. 2008. How green are biofuels? *Science* **319**: 43-44.

Sempik, J., Aldridge, J. & Becker, A. 2005. *Growing Together: a Practical Guide to Promoting Social Inclusion through Gardening and Horticulture.* Policy Press, Bristol, UK.

Simpson, S. & Straus, M. C. 1997. *Horticulture as Therapy: Principles and Practice.* Food Products Press, Philadelphia, PA.

Socolow, R., Hotinski, R., Greenblatt, J. B. & Pacala, S. 2004. Solving the climate problem: technologies available to curb $CO_2$ emissions. *Environment* **46**: 8-19.

Stephen, W. (ed.). 2004. *Think Global, Act Local: the Life and Legacy of Patrick Geddes.* Luath Press Ltd., Edinburgh, UK.

Stern, N. 2007. *The Economics of Climate Change: the Stern Review.* Cambridge University Press, Cambridge, UK.

Stringer, C. B. & Andrews, P. 2005. *The Complete World of Human Evolution.* Thames & Hudson Ltd., London, UK.

Tickell, O. 2008. *Kyoto 2: How to Manage the Global Greenhouse.* Zed Books Ltd., London, UK.

Wilson, E. O. 1992. *The Diversity of Life.* Allen Lane, London, UK.

Wilson, E. O. 2002. *The Future of Life.* Knopf, New York.

Wilson, E. O. 2007. *The Creation: an Appeal to Save Life on Earth.* Norton, New York.

Van Wyck, B.-E. 2005. *Food Plants of the World: an Illustrated Guide.* Timber Press, Portland, OR.

# Websites and on-line materials

## Biodiversity:

Food and Agriculture Organisation (FAO) 2007. *State of the World's Forests 2007:* www.fao.org/docrep/009/a0773e/a0773e00.htm

Integrated Taxonomic Information System: www.itis.gov

International Plant Names Index: www.ipni.org

Millennium Ecosystem Assessment: www.millenniumassessment.org

The Global Strategy for Plant Conservation: www.plants2010.org

Soil biodiversity - NERC's Sourhope website at http://soilbio.nerc.ac.uk/Sourhope.htm

*The Economics of Ecosystems and Biodiversity: Interim Report:* http://ec.europa.eu/environment/nature/biodiversity/economics/pdf/teeb_report.pdf.

The Biodiversity Convention: www.cbd.int

The Global Strategy for Plant Conservation: www.bgci.org/ourwork/gspc

UK Biodiversity Action Plan and species Action Plans: www.ukbap.org.uk

World Conservation Union: www.iucn.org with their "Red List of Threatened Species" at http://www.iucnredlist.org/

## Climate change:

BBC News climate change web-page: http://news.bbc.co.uk/1/hi/sci/tech/portal/climate_change/default.stm

Defra's climate change web page: http://www.defra.gov.uk/environment/climatechange/internat/index.htm

European Commission climate change web-page: http://www.climatechange.eu.com/

Intergovernmental Panel on Climate Change: www.ipcc.ch

Met Office: www.metoffice.gov.uk/climatechange/

National Geographic: http://environment.nationalgeographic.com/environment/global-warming/gw-overview.html

Our Future Planet: http://www.ourfutureplanet.org/

Princeton University Stabilization Wedges: www.princeton.edu/~cmi/resources/stabwedge.htm

Royal Society. 2005. *A Guide to Facts and Fictions About Climate Change:* http://royalsociety.org/downloaddoc.asp?id=1630

Scottish Government *2008 Climate Change Consultation on Proposals for a Scottish Climate Change Bill: Scottish Government Response:* www.scotland.gov.uk/Resource/Doc/921/0067463.pdf

Stern Report: www.hm-treasury.gov.uk/sternreview_index.htm

United Nations Environment Programme: www.unep.org/themes/climatechange

UK Committee on Climate Change: www.theccc.org.uk

UK Climate Impacts Programme: www.ukcip.org.uk/index.php

UK Government Office of Climate Change: www.occ.gov.uk/activities/stern.htm

## Organisations:

Botanic Gardens Conservation International: www.bgci.org

Caledonian Forest website at Trees for Life: www.treesforlife.org.uk

Consortium for the Barcode of Life: www.barcoding.si.edu

Forestry Commission: www.forestry.gov.uk

International Conifer Conservation Programme: www.rbge.org.uk/science/genetics-and-conservation/international-conifer-conservation-programme

Millennium Forest for Scotland: www.millenniumforest.co.uk

Plantlife: www.plantlife.org.uk

*The Global Strategy for Plant Conservation:* www.cbd.int/gspc/

*The Gran Canaria Declaration: Calling for a Global Program for Plant Conservation:* www.cbd.int/doc/meetings/cop/cop-05/information/cop-05-inf-32-en.pdf

World Lands Trust: www.worldlandtrust.org

## Patrick Geddes:

www.ballaterscotland.com/geddes/

www.patrickgeddestrust.co.uk/

"By leaves we live" from Patrick Geddes' farewell
        lecture to his Dundee students is reproduced
        in part at www.dundee.ac.uk/main/about
        patrick_geddes.htm.

## Royal Botanic Garden Edinburgh

RBGE website: www.rbge.org.uk

PlantNetwork Target 8 Project at the Royal Botanic
        Garden Edinburgh: www.rbge.org.uk/science/
        conservation/plantnetwork-target-8-project

Scottish Plants Project at the Royal Botanic Garden
        Edinburgh: www.rbge.org.uk/science/
        genetics-and-conservation/Conservation-and-
        Ecology/Scottish-Plants-Project

Royal Botanic Garden Edinburgh web-page on DNA
        barcoding at www.rbge.org.uk/science/
        genetics-and-conservation/Molecular-
        Ecology/dna-barcoding

Royal Botanic Garden Edinburgh web-page on the
        John Hope Gateway at www.rbge.org.uk/the-
        gardens/edinburgh/the-gateway

## Sustainable living:

Biofuelwatch: www.biofuelwatch.org.uk

Eartheasy: www.eartheasy.com

EnviroLink: www.envirolink.org

One Planet Living:
        www.oneplanetliving.org/index.html

The UK government's approach to sustainable
        development: www.defra.gov.uk/sustainable/
        government/

The UK's independent watchdog on sustainable
        development: www.sd-commission.org.uk

World Bank Millennium Development Goals:
        http://devdata.worldbank.org/atlas-mdg/

## Acknowledgements

I am grateful to Alan Bennell, Shauna Hay and Sara Oldfield for encouraging me to develop the ideas expressed here into book form.

I thank Fay Young for her enthusiastic support whilst editing the text with great sensitivity and Alexandra Wortley for helping to check facts and track down literature.

I feel deeply honoured that His Royal Highness The Prince of Wales kindly provided a Foreword.

I am indebted to all those who have provided illustrations and to Hamish Adamson, Sarah Batey, Ida Maspero and Joanna MacGregor for their work in bringing this book to publication.

Finally, I am grateful to the following for the use of illustrations in the background of some pages throughout this book: Isik Güner; Mary Mendum; Shire Publications Ltd; Rosemary Wise.

# INDEX